sizzling

delicious

flames

spices

juicy

smoking

barbecue

the essential grilling, rub, and marinade recipes

Love Food ™ is an imprint of Parragon Books Ltd

Parragon
Queen Street House
4 Queen Street
Bath BA1 1HE, UK

Photography by Günter Beer
Home Economist Stevan Paul
Design by Talking Design
Introduction by Anna Brandenburger

Copyright © Parragon Books Ltd 2007

Love Food ™ and the accompanying heart device is a trademark of Parragon Books Ltd

ISBN: 978-1-4054-9242-3

Printed in China

This book uses imperial, metric, and US cup measurements. Follow the same units of measurement throughout; do not mix metric and imperial. All spoon measurements are level, unless otherwise stated: teaspoons are assumed to be 5 ml and tablespoons are assumed to be 15 ml. Unless otherwise stated, milk is assumed to be whole, eggs and individual fruits such as bananas are medium, and pepper is freshly ground black pepper.

Recipes using raw or very lightly cooked eggs should be avoided by infants, the elderly, pregnant women, convalescents, and anyone suffering from an illness. Pregnant and breast-feeding women are advised to avoid eating peanuts and peanut products.

CONTENTS

Introduction

You know summer has arrived when the familiar smell of charcoal smoke starts wafting over backyards. As the gloom of cold wet winter days disappears and the sun gains its strength, our natural inclination is to spend as much time outdoors as possible. Cooking and entertaining with a barbecue is the obvious choice when it is either too warm to fire up the indoor oven or you simply want to be able to spend more time socializing while cooking.

Simple food—and lots of it—is the best: a plain steak is totally transformed on a grill and given a smoky, earthy flavor. An important point to remember is that everything tastes better in the fresh air and the delicious cooking smells only add to the hunger level, which means that everyone's appetite somehow increases when eating outside.

Barbecues need not be limited just to the backyard or patio; you can easily take a portable or disposable grill along on your camping trip, picnic on the beach, or even up a mountain. With just a little forward planning you can easily cook up a feast wherever you choose.

As well as the actual grilled food, do not forget all the extras. In this book there is a wealth of sumptuous salads, sauces, and wonderful desserts that all add to the occasion. Try some of the cocktails—both alcoholic and nonalcoholic—guaranteed to get the party started.

Getting Started

Choosing a barbecue grill

There are so many different sorts of grills on the market it is often a daunting task to know where to begin. You can find everything from the disposable filled aluminum tray in markets and garages, all the way up to the extremely sophisticated gas grills that light at the flick of a switch and come with masses of gadgets and dials. A good way to start your search is to think about how and when you are likely to use the grill. If you live in an area where you know your climate is only likely to afford you a few warm weekends, do not think too big. If, on the other hand, you have a large family or enjoy entertaining, a small kettle grill will definitely not suffice and it might even be worth building your own brick grill.

One of the first choices to make is whether you want to use gas or charcoal for heat. This is more of a lifestyle choice. If you are convinced that food cooked over hot charcoal has the best flavor and take pride in getting the fire started then charcoal is for you. Alternatively, if you want the perfect fire at the touch of a button and to be able to control the temperature then a gas grill is the ideal choice.

Charcoal grills

The **kettle grill** comes with a lid which is great for cooking larger pieces of meat, or even whole birds, by keeping in the heat. It also means that if the rain decides to start at just the wrong time, you can continue cooking. These are sturdy pieces of equipment that often come with wheels for easy mobility.

Flat-bed grills often have a larger area for cooking and sometimes come with varying levels on which to fit the grill racks. This is useful when cooking a large amount of food as you can move food that is nearly cooked up to a higher rack.

Brick or masonry **built-in grills** are great if you have a large yard and really enjoy grilling on a regular basis. They can be built to your own simple design using household bricks and a sturdy metal tray and rack. Alternatively there are many ready-built or DIY kits available.

Portable charcoal grills come in a variety of shapes and are usually made to fold closed for easy carrying. They also usually come with legs to attach while cooking so the hot base is not directly on the ground.

Disposable grills cost just a few dollars from stores and garages. They are perfect for picnics and the occasional backyard cook-out. They are very easy to use and heat up in a matter of minutes, although do not stay hot for very long so are really only good for foods that cook quickly. They come in various sizes depending on how much food you have to cook. They are also good for keeping vegetarian food separate.

Gas grills

Gas grills run from the basic grill with an area below to store the gas cylinder, all the way up to a huge 6-burner mega-contraption with pan hot plates on one side, a rotisserie area, and warming ovens. They all have covers that easily lift and lower and come with wheels so you can position them where you like. The choice is really down to the size of your budget.

Portable gas grills offer the easiest way to cook up a great meal while out and about. They are neat and compact, if a little heavy, and have all the speed and convenience of their larger cousins.

Fuel types

Charcoal briquettes are the most common type of fuel for charcoal grills. They are often made from sawdust, wood scraps, and binders with chemicals added to enhance burning. Some briquettes are impregnated with a lighting agent and sold in bags as **instant lighting charcoal**. These bags are placed directly into the grill and the bag itself is lit.

Hardwood charcoal is natural additive-free wood chunks that have been carbonized in an oxygen-free oven. The advantage of these is that they burn cleanly and somewhat hotter than the briquettes, but they sometimes give out sparks at first.

Woodchips for grills are generally made from hardwood and their aroma is wonderful, but they can be difficult to get started. They can lose their heat sooner than charcoal so are suitable when cooking small amounts of food. Some woodchips are "flavored" with hickory or mesquite which gives the food a delicious flavor. If the chips are first soaked for 30 to 60 minutes in water, they will gently smoke rather than catch light.

Grilling food directly over just **wood** is a little more difficult. This is because the wood burns fiercely for a shorter time and then cools rapidly. If you do choose this fuel, however, opt for apple, oak, or cherry and avoid pine as it exudes noxious smoke that will ruin the food.

Gas grills take **propane** or **butane gas** in various sizes of bottles and cylinders. They generally fit underneath the grill area and have secure valves to shut off the gas supply once you have finished cooking. Always store gas cylinders or bottles outside and protect them from direct sunlight and frost. It is not advisable to keep more spare cylinders than you need. The bottles and cylinders can be ordered from gas suppliers who will deliver them or they can be bought from large homeware stores.

Tips for getting started

Lighting a charcoal grill is not difficult, but there are a few general rules to follow. First, keep the charcoal briquettes dry, preferably in an airtight container, to help the charcoal light faster. Place the briquettes in a pyramid in the center of the grill. If you are using barbecue lighter fluid, douse this evenly over the briquettes and allow to soak in for a few minutes. If using barbecue fire lighters, poke these between the briquettes about a third of the way up the pyramid. Using long kitchen matches, either light the doused briquettes or the fire lighters. The charcoal will take about 30 minutes to get hot. Once the briquettes start to get hot, they will glow a red to orange color, then gradually turn a whitish gray. It is the white ash over the coals that tells you that they are really hot. Now you can spread them out evenly over the bottom of the grill. Do not worry if some of the coals from the center of the pyramid are still orange—just give them a few more minutes to turn gray too. Place the grill rack over the top. It is a good idea to wait a few more minutes before adding the food, in order to allow the rack to heat up really well.

If you are cooking over wood, a similar principal applies as to charcoal. These fires start up best by using barbecue fire lighters tucked in between the pieces of wood. Again, light the blocks of wood in a pyramid and when they are burning well, and the flames have subsided a little, spread them out to an even layer and place the metal grill on top.

Gas grills are the easiest of all to light. Depending on your model, there are a variety of controls (refer to your manufacturer's guidelines). It is usually best to light the grill to its hottest setting and then reduce the heat as needed. First open the grill lid, then the gas tank. Allow 2 to 3 seconds for the gas chamber to fill, then push the ignite button. Once all the burners are lit, close the lid to allow it to preheat. When hot, place the food on the grate, and adjust the burners to the desired heat.

Useful equipment

There are masses of grilling gadgets on the market, but only a few of these are really necessary:

Tongs are probably the most important tool you will need, so it is important to have a good sturdy pair that will grasp the food well and save you from burning your fingers.

Oven mitts are a good idea if you have a large grill and have to reach over the hot coals.

Basting brushes allow you to marinate your food, adding flavor and moisture, as it cooks.

Wooden or metal skewers are a good idea when grilling smaller items. If you choose wooden skewers, make sure that you soak them in water for at least 30 minutes before using so they do not catch on fire.

Hinged wire racks make cooking less stable items, such as fish or homemade burgers, much easier. Smaller items can be cooked together and turned all at the same time which allows for more even cooking.

Meat thermometers are essential if you are cooking a large piece of meat as it can be difficult to judge whether it is cooked through.

Long handled spatulas are great for turning food and removing it once cooked.

An **oil spray** can be used to spray the grill rack or flat plate before cooking to prevent the food from sticking.

A **wire brush** is useful for removing any burnt-on debris from the grill rack during and after use. For the best results, clean while the rack is still warm.

Fire and food safety

Once you have decided which type of grill to buy, the next step is to choose the site. It is crucial that the barbecue is placed on level ground where it cannot wobble or tip over—this makes cooking easier as well as safer. For fire safety, make sure the grill is a good distance from any houses, sheds, fences, or overhanging trees. A sheltered position will help the grill heat up more evenly and cut down on smoke blowing about. Keep a bucket of water or a fire blanket nearby and never leave a hot grill unattended.

Once the barbecue has done its work, allow it to cool completely. With charcoal grills, the cool ash can be disposed of by tipping it onto bare garden soil or into a plastic bag and then into the trash can.

For a healthy barbecue, there are a few points to remember about food storage, preparation, and cooking:

- All frozen food must be completely defrosted before cooking.
- Store uncooked meat, poultry, and fish in airtight containers in the refrigerator. For a large party or picnic, invest in a cooler. It is best to return raw foods to room temperature for about 1 hour before cooking.
- Use different chopping boards and utensils for raw and cooked foods.
- Do not put raw and nearly-cooked meat next to each other on the grill.
- Poultry should be cooked thoroughly so that no pink remains.
- Do not crowd the grill—allow 1 inch between items.
- If the marinade you are using for basting has been in contact with raw meat, poultry, or seafood, make sure that you do not use it during the last few minutes of cooking because any harmful bacteria may not be destroyed by the heat of the grill. The safest way is to reserve a portion of the marinade for basting before adding raw foods.

Tips for the perfect barbecue party

Gathering around the backyard grill is not usually a formal occasion. However, a certain amount of careful planning and smartening up of the yard or deck will create the perfect party atmosphere and ensure that everything runs smoothly.

Here are some ideas to help:

- Have plenty of disposable plates, glasses, and cutlery on hand. Even if you plan to use your regular crockery and cutlery, they are always useful for extra guests or small children.
- Serve potato chips and snacks in bowls placed around the yard or deck so guests are happy to spread out and do not all hover in one area.
- Find a good spot to place a large tub of ice, and fill it with bottles and cans of drink. Guests will be able to help themselves to drinks, saving you the job of refilling everyone's glasses. Remember the bottle openers and corkscrews!
- Provide a good supply of nonalcoholic drinks. If the party is running for quite a few hours on a hot afternoon, people are going to drink quite a lot and will not want just alcoholic drinks.
- See if you can find or borrow outdoor games for children of all ages to keep them occupied and happy.

- Appetites are always enhanced when eating outdoors so plan on larger portions than usual.
- Aim for two or three different main course choices and have lots of salads and bread on hand so people can help themselves.
- Make sure you have enough non-meat items for any vegetarian guests.
- If you are entertaining a crowd and think your grill might not be big enough to cook all the food at once, you can precook some in the oven. Then reheat it on the grill to give it that wonderful smoky flavor and crispy skin; just make sure it is piping hot all the way through.

Countdown to a barbecue party:

1 week ahead
- If you have a gas grill, check that the gas cylinder is full and the valves in good working order. If your cylinder is less than half full, order a full one to use for the party. With a charcoal grill, check you have enough charcoal and lighting agent.
- Rent or borrow glasses if necessary.
- Count up guest numbers and chase up any guests who have not responded.
- Find out if any of your guests have special dietary requirements and plan what you are going to cook.
- Shop for non-perishable items, such as drinks, chips, sauces, and relishes. Remember to stock up on trash bags!
- Check that outdoor furniture is in good condition and you have enough chairs, table cloths, napkins, and serving platters. If it is an evening party, shop for candles, garden lanterns, and insect repellent.

1 day ahead
- Shop for meat, poultry, fish, fresh fruit, and vegetables.
- Marinate meat, poultry, or fish, as well as vegetables, and prepare side dishes and sauces. Start to prepare desserts that can be made ahead and stored.
- Clear space in the refrigerator for drinks and salads.
- Have a last minute tidy up around the yard and make sure your plants and lawn are well watered. Sweep and clean up patio or deck areas.
- Check the weather forecast and make indoor plans if there is a good chance of rain. If weather permits, set up chairs and tables outside.

On the day
- Buy ice and place in a large container to keep drinks cool and free up refrigerator space.
- Prepare salads (do not add dressing until serving) and put finishing touches to side dishes and desserts.

1 hour ahead
- Prepare the grill for lighting.
- Remove marinated food from the refrigerator to allow it to come to room temperature.

Barbecue Classics

boozy beef steaks

serves 4

4 beef steaks
4 tbsp whiskey or brandy
2 tbsp soy sauce
1 tbsp dark brown sugar
pepper
tomato slices
fresh parsley sprigs,
 to garnish
garlic bread, to serve

Make a few cuts in the edge of the fat on each steak. This will stop the meat curling as it cooks. Place the meat in a shallow, nonmetallic dish.

Mix the whiskey, soy sauce, sugar, and pepper to taste together in a small bowl, stirring until the sugar dissolves. Pour the mixture over the steak. Cover with plastic wrap and let marinate in the refrigerator for at least 2 hours.

Preheat the barbecue. Cook the beef steaks over hot coals, searing the meat over the hottest part of the grill for 2 minutes on each side.

Move the meat to an area with slightly less intense heat and cook for an additional 4–10 minutes on each side, depending on how well done you like your steaks. To test if the meat is cooked, insert the point of a sharp knife into the meat—the juices will run from red when the meat is still rare, to clear as it becomes well cooked.

Lightly grill the tomato slices for 1–2 minutes. Transfer the meat and the tomatoes to warmed serving plates. Garnish with fresh parsley sprigs and serve with garlic bread.

a sizzling dish with a touch of spice

barbecued steak fajitas

· ·

serves 4

2 tbsp corn oil, plus extra
    for oiling
finely grated rind of 1 lime
1 tbsp lime juice
2 garlic cloves, crushed
¼ tsp ground coriander
¼ tsp ground cumin
pinch of sugar
salt and pepper
1 piece of sirloin or top
    round, about 1 lb 8 oz/
    675 g and ¾ inch/2 cm
    thick
4 flour tortillas
1 avocado
2 tomatoes, thinly sliced
4 tbsp sour cream
4 scallions, thinly sliced

To make the marinade, put the oil, lime rind and juice, garlic, coriander, cumin, sugar, and salt and pepper to taste into a large, shallow, nonmetallic dish large enough to hold the steak and mix together. Add the steak and turn in the marinade to coat it. Cover and let marinate in the refrigerator for 6–8 hours or up to 24 hours, turning occasionally.

When ready to cook, preheat the barbecue. Using a slotted spoon, remove the steak from the marinade, put onto the grill rack, and cook over medium heat for 5 minutes for rare or 8–10 minutes for medium, turning the steak frequently and basting once or twice with any remaining marinade.

Meanwhile, warm the tortillas according to the instructions on the package. Peel, pit, and slice the avocado.

Thinly slice the steak across the grain and arrange an equal quantity of the slices on one side of each tortilla. Add the tomato and avocado slices, top with a spoonful of sour cream, and sprinkle over the scallions. Fold over and eat at once.

barbecued pork sausages with thyme

serves 4

1 garlic clove, finely
  chopped
1 onion, grated
1 small red chile, seeded
  and finely chopped
1 lb/450 g lean ground
  pork
scant ⅔ cup almonds,
  toasted and ground
1 cup fresh breadcrumbs
1 tbsp finely chopped
  fresh thyme
salt and pepper
flour, for dusting
vegetable oil, for brushing

to serve
fresh hotdog rolls
slices of onion,
  lightly cooked
ketchup and/or mustard

Put the garlic, onion, chile, pork, almonds, breadcrumbs, and thyme into a large bowl. Season well with salt and pepper and mix until well combined.

Using your hands, form the mixture into sausage shapes. Roll each sausage in a little flour, then transfer to a bowl, cover with plastic wrap, and let chill for 45 minutes.

Preheat the barbecue. Brush a piece of aluminum foil with oil, then put the sausages on the foil and brush them with a little more vegetable oil. Transfer the sausages and foil to the barbecue.

Barbecue over hot coals, turning the sausages frequently, for about 15 minutes, or until cooked through. Serve with hotdog rolls, cooked sliced onion, and ketchup and/or mustard.

these tangy ribs will disappear in minutes

hot & spicy ribs

serves 4

1 onion, chopped
2 garlic cloves, chopped
1-inch/2.5-cm piece
   fresh gingerroot, sliced
1 fresh red chile, seeded
   and chopped
5 tbsp dark soy sauce
3 tbsp lime juice
1 tbsp brown sugar
2 tbsp peanut oil
salt and pepper
2 lb 4 oz/1 kg pork
   spareribs, separated

Preheat the barbecue. Put the onion, garlic, ginger, chile, and soy sauce into a food processor and process to a paste. Transfer to a measuring cup and stir in the lime juice, sugar, and oil. Season with salt and pepper.

Place the spareribs in a preheated wok or large, heavy-bottom pan and pour in the soy sauce mixture. Place on the stove and bring to a boil, then let simmer over low heat, stirring frequently, for 30 minutes. If the mixture appears to be drying out, add a little water.

Remove the spareribs, reserving the sauce. Cook the ribs over medium hot coals, turning and basting frequently with the sauce, for 20–30 minutes. Transfer to a large serving plate and serve immediately.

pork with a wonderfully messy sticky glaze

honey-glazed
pork chops

· ·

serves 4

4 lean pork loin chops
salt and pepper
4 tbsp clear honey
1 tbsp dry sherry
4 tbsp orange juice
2 tbsp olive oil
1-inch/2.5-cm piece
   fresh gingerroot, grated
corn oil, for oiling

Preheat the barbecue. Season the pork chops with salt and pepper to taste. Reserve while you make the glaze.

To make the glaze, place the honey, sherry, orange juice, olive oil, and gingerroot in a small pan and heat gently, stirring constantly, until well blended.

Cook the pork chops on an oiled rack over hot coals for 5 minutes on each side.

Brush the chops with the glaze and cook for an additional 2–4 minutes on each side, basting frequently with the glaze.

Transfer the pork chops to warmed serving plates and serve hot.

the spicy marinade gives lamb a whole new dimension

spicy lamb steaks

serves 4

4 lamb steaks, about
   6 oz/175 g each
8 fresh rosemary sprigs
8 fresh bay leaves
2 tbsp olive oil

spicy marinade
2 tbsp corn oil
1 large onion,
   finely chopped
2 garlic cloves,
   finely chopped
2 tbsp Jamaican jerk
   seasoning
1 tbsp curry paste
1 tsp grated fresh
   gingerroot
14 oz/400 g canned
   chopped tomatoes
4 tbsp Worcestershire
   sauce
3 tbsp light brown sugar
salt and pepper

To make the marinade, heat the oil in a heavy-bottom pan. Add the onion and garlic and cook, stirring occasionally, for 5 minutes, or until softened. Stir in the jerk seasoning, curry paste, and grated ginger, and cook, stirring constantly, for 2 minutes. Add the tomatoes, Worcestershire sauce, and sugar, then season to taste with salt and pepper. Bring to a boil, stirring constantly, then reduce the heat and let simmer for 15 minutes, or until thickened. Remove from the heat and let cool.

Place the lamb steaks between 2 sheets of plastic wrap and beat with the side of a rolling pin to flatten. Transfer the steaks to a large, shallow, nonmetallic dish. Pour the marinade over them, turning to coat. Cover with plastic wrap and let marinate in the refrigerator for 3 hours.

Preheat the barbecue. Drain the lamb, reserving the marinade. Cook the lamb over medium hot coals, brushing frequently with the marinade, for 5–7 minutes on each side. Meanwhile, dip the rosemary and bay leaves in the olive oil and cook on the barbecue for 3–5 minutes. Serve the lamb immediately with the herbs.

spiced lamb chops with cooling
minty yogurt

minted lamb chops

serves 6

6 lamb chops, about
   6 oz/175 g each
⅔ cup strained plain
   yogurt
2 garlic cloves, finely
   chopped
1 tsp grated fresh
   gingerroot
¼ tsp coriander seeds,
   crushed
salt and pepper
1 tbsp olive oil, plus extra
   for brushing
1 tbsp orange juice
1 tsp walnut oil
2 tbsp chopped fresh mint

Place the chops in a large, shallow, nonmetallic bowl. Mix half the yogurt, the garlic, ginger, and coriander seeds together in a measuring cup and season to taste with salt and pepper. Spoon the mixture over the chops, turning to coat, then cover with plastic wrap and let marinate in the refrigerator for 2 hours, turning occasionally.

Preheat the barbecue. Place the remaining yogurt, the olive oil, orange juice, walnut oil, and mint in a small bowl and, using a handheld blender, mix until thoroughly blended. Season to taste with salt and pepper. Cover the minted yogurt with plastic wrap and let chill in the refrigerator until ready to serve.

Drain the chops, scraping off the marinade. Brush with olive oil and cook over medium hot coals for 5–7 minutes on each side. Serve immediately with the minted yogurt.

this barbecue favorite is sure
to be a hit

cajun chicken

• •

serves 4

4 chicken drumsticks
4 chicken thighs
2 fresh corn cobs, husks
   and silks removed
3 oz/85 g butter, melted

spice mix
2 tsp onion powder
2 tsp paprika
1½ tsp salt
1 tsp garlic powder
1 tsp dried thyme
1 tsp cayenne pepper
1 tsp ground black pepper
½ tsp ground white pepper
¼ tsp ground cumin

Preheat the barbecue. Using a sharp knife, make 2–3 diagonal slashes in the chicken drumsticks and thighs, then place them in a large dish. Cut the corn cobs into thick slices and add them to the dish. Mix all the ingredients for the spice mix together in a small bowl.

Brush the chicken and corn with the melted butter and sprinkle with the spice mix. Toss to coat well.

Cook the chicken over medium hot coals, turning occasionally, for 15 minutes, then add the corn slices and cook, turning occasionally, for an additional 10–15 minutes, or until starting to blacken slightly at the edges. Transfer to a large serving plate and serve immediately.

spicy chicken wings

serves 4

16 chicken wings
4 tbsp corn oil
4 tbsp light soy sauce
2-inch/5-cm piece of fresh
  gingerroot, coarsely
  chopped
2 garlic cloves, coarsely
  chopped
juice and grated rind of
  1 lemon
2 tsp ground cinnamon
2 tsp ground turmeric
4 tbsp honey
salt and pepper

sauce
2 orange bell peppers
2 yellow bell peppers
corn oil, for brushing
½ cup plain yogurt
2 tbsp dark soy sauce
2 tbsp chopped fresh
  cilantro

Place the chicken wings in a large, shallow, nonmetallic dish. Put the oil, soy sauce, ginger, garlic, lemon rind and juice, cinnamon, turmeric, and honey into a food processor and process to a smooth purée. Season to taste with salt and pepper. Spoon the mixture over the chicken wings and turn until thoroughly coated, cover with plastic wrap and let marinate in the refrigerator for up to 8 hours.

Preheat the barbecue. To make the sauce, brush the bell peppers with the oil and cook over hot coals, turning frequently, for 10 minutes, or until the skin is blackened and charred. Remove from the barbecue and let cool slightly, then remove the skins and discard the seeds. Put the flesh into a food processor with the yogurt and process to a smooth purée. Transfer to a bowl and stir in the soy sauce and chopped cilantro.

Drain the chicken wings, reserving the marinade. Cook over medium hot coals, turning and brushing frequently with the reserved marinade, for 8–10 minutes, or until thoroughly cooked. Serve immediately with the sauce.

perhaps one of the best-known Caribbean dishes

jerk chicken

serves 4

4 lean chicken parts
1 bunch of scallions,
    trimmed
1–2 chiles (Scotch bonnet,
    if possible)
1 garlic clove
2-inch/5-cm piece of fresh
    gingerroot, peeled and
    roughly chopped
½ tsp dried thyme
½ tsp paprika
¼ tsp ground allspice
pinch ground cinnamon
pinch ground cloves
4 tbsp white wine vinegar
3 tbsp light soy sauce
pepper

Rinse the chicken parts and pat them dry on paper towels. Place them in a shallow dish.

Place the scallions, chiles, garlic, ginger, thyme, paprika, allspice, cinnamon, cloves, wine vinegar, soy sauce, and pepper to taste in a food processor and process until smooth.

Pour the spicy mixture over the chicken. Turn the chicken parts over so that they are well coated in the marinade.

Transfer the chicken parts to the refrigerator and leave to marinate for up to 24 hours.

Remove the chicken from the marinade and grill over medium hot coals for about 30 minutes, turning the chicken over and basting occasionally with any remaining marinade, until the chicken is browned and cooked through.

Transfer the chicken parts to individual serving plates and serve at once.

chicken with a piquant sweet-and-sour glaze

mustard & honey
drumsticks

∙∙∙

serves 4

8 chicken drumsticks
salad greens, to serve

glaze
½ cup honey
4 tbsp Dijon mustard
4 tbsp whole-grain
    mustard
4 tbsp white wine vinegar
2 tbsp corn oil
salt and pepper

Using a sharp knife, make 2–3 diagonal slashes in the chicken drumsticks and place them in a large, nonmetallic dish.

Mix all the ingredients for the glaze together in a measuring cup and season to taste with salt and pepper. Pour the glaze over the drumsticks, turning until the drumsticks are well coated. Cover with plastic wrap and let marinate in the refrigerator for at least 1 hour.

Preheat the barbecue. Drain the chicken drumsticks, reserving the marinade. Cook the chicken over medium hot coals, turning frequently and brushing with the reserved marinade, for 25–30 minutes, or until thoroughly cooked. Transfer to serving plates and serve immediately with the salad greens.

this wonderfully aromatic rub is perfect with fish

charred **fish**

serves 4

4 whitefish steaks
1 tbsp paprika
1 tsp dried thyme
1 tsp cayenne pepper
1 tsp black pepper
½ tsp white pepper
½ tsp salt
¼ tsp ground allspice
1¾ oz/50 g unsalted butter
3 tbsp corn oil
green beans, to serve

Preheat the barbecue. Rinse the fish steaks under cold running water and pat dry with paper towels.

Mix the paprika, thyme, cayenne, black and white peppers, salt, and ground allspice together in a shallow dish.

Place the butter and corn oil in a small pan and heat gently, stirring occasionally, until the butter melts.

Brush the butter mixture liberally all over the fish steaks, on both sides, then dip the fish into the spicy mix until coated on both sides.

Cook the fish over hot coals for 5 minutes on each side until cooked through. Continue to baste the fish with the remaining butter mixture during the cooking time. Serve with the green beans.

salmon
with mango salsa

serves 4

4 salmon steaks, about
   6 oz/175 g each
finely grated rind
   and juice of 1 lime or
   ½ lemon
salt and pepper

salsa
1 large mango, peeled,
   seeded, and diced
1 red onion, finely chopped
2 passion fruit
2 fresh basil sprigs
2 tbsp lime juice
salt

Preheat the barbecue. Rinse the salmon steaks under cold running water, pat dry with paper towels, and place in a large, shallow, nonmetallic dish. Sprinkle with the lime rind and pour the juice over them. Season to taste with salt and pepper, cover, and let stand while you make the salsa.

Place the mango flesh in a bowl with the onion. Cut the passion fruit in half and scoop out the seeds and pulp with a teaspoon into the bowl. Tear the basil leaves and add them to the bowl with the lime juice. Season to taste with salt and stir. Cover with plastic wrap and set aside until required.

Cook the salmon steaks over medium hot coals for 3–4 minutes on each side. Serve immediately with the salsa.

citrus tuna with a spicy sauce on the side

charbroiled tuna with chile salsa

· ·

serves 4

4 tuna steaks, about
  6 oz/175 g each
grated rind and juice
  of 1 lime
2 tbsp olive oil
salt and pepper
fresh cilantro sprigs,
  to garnish
lettuce leaves, to garnish
crusty bread, to serve

chile salsa
2 orange bell peppers
1 tbsp olive oil
juice of 1 lime
juice of 1 orange
2–3 fresh red chiles,
  seeded and chopped
pinch of cayenne pepper

Rinse the tuna thoroughly under cold running water and pat dry with paper towels, then place in a large, shallow, nonmetallic dish. Sprinkle with the lime rind and pour the juice and olive oil over the fish. Season to taste with salt and pepper, cover with plastic wrap, and let marinate in the refrigerator for up to 1 hour.

Preheat the barbecue. To make the salsa, brush the bell peppers with the olive oil and cook over hot coals, turning frequently, for 10 minutes, or until the skin is blackened and charred. Remove from the barbecue and let cool slightly, then remove the skins and discard the seeds. Put the bell peppers into a food processor with the remaining salsa ingredients and process to a purée. Transfer to a bowl and season to taste with salt and pepper.

Cook the tuna over hot coals for 4–5 minutes on each side, until golden. Transfer to serving plates, garnish with cilantro sprigs and lettuce leaves, and serve with the salsa and plenty of crusty bread.

this tasty treat is great for vegetarians

eggplant & mozzarella
sandwiches

∙∙

serves 2

1 large eggplant
1 tbsp lemon juice
3 tbsp olive oil
salt and pepper
1¼ cups grated mozzarella
  cheese
2 sun-dried tomatoes,
  chopped

to serve
Italian bread
mixed salad greens
tomato slices

Preheat the barbecue. Using a sharp knife, slice the eggplant into thin rounds.

Mix the lemon juice and olive oil together in a small bowl and season the mixture with salt and pepper to taste. Brush the eggplant slices with the olive oil and lemon juice mixture and cook over medium hot coals for 2–3 minutes, without turning, until golden on the underside.

Turn half of the eggplant slices over and sprinkle with cheese and chopped sun-dried tomatoes.

Place the remaining eggplant slices on top of the cheese and tomatoes, turning them so that the pale side is facing up. Cook for 1–2 minutes, then carefully turn the whole sandwich over and cook for an additional 1–2 minutes. Baste with the olive oil mixture.

Serve in Italian bread with mixed salad greens and a few slices of tomato.

a delicious mix of vegetables, beans, and cheese

vegetarian
sausages

∙ ∙

serves 4

1 tbsp corn oil,
   plus extra for oiling
1 small onion, finely
   chopped
2 oz/50 g button
   mushrooms, finely
   chopped
½ red bell pepper, seeded
   and finely chopped
14 oz/400 g canned
   cannellini beans, rinsed
   and drained
2 cups fresh breadcrumbs
1 cup grated Cheddar
   cheese
1 tsp dried mixed herbs
1 egg yolk
seasoned all-purpose flour

to serve
small bread rolls
fried onion slices
tomato chutney

Heat the corn oil in a pan. Add the onion, mushrooms, and bell pepper, and cook until softened.

Mash the cannellini beans in a large bowl. Add the onion, mushroom, and bell pepper mixture, and the breadcrumbs, cheese, herbs, and egg yolk and mix well. Press the mixture together with your fingers and shape into 8 sausages. Roll each sausage in the seasoned flour. Chill in the refrigerator for at least 30 minutes.

Preheat the barbecue. Cook the sausages on a sheet of oiled aluminum foil set over medium hot coals for 15–20 minutes, turning and basting frequently with oil, until golden. Split the bread rolls down the center and insert a layer of cooked onions. Place the sausages in the rolls and serve with tomato chutney.

Entertaining

beef
with wild mushrooms

serves 4

4 beef steaks
1¾ oz/50 g butter
1–2 garlic cloves, crushed
5½ oz/150 g mixed wild
    mushrooms
2 tbsp chopped fresh
    parsley

to serve
salad greens
cherry tomatoes, halved

Preheat the barbecue. Place the steaks onto a cutting board and using a sharp knife, cut a pocket into the side of each steak.

To make the stuffing, heat the butter in a large skillet. Add the garlic and cook gently for 1 minute. Add the mushrooms to the skillet and cook gently for 4–6 minutes, or until tender. Remove the skillet from the heat and stir in the parsley.

Divide the mushroom mixture into 4 and insert a portion into the pocket of each steak. Seal the pocket with a toothpick. If preparing ahead, allow the mixture to cool before stuffing the steaks.

Cook the steaks over hot coals, searing the meat over the hottest part of the grill for 2 minutes on each side. Move the steaks to an area with slightly less intense heat and cook for an additional 4–10 minutes on each side, depending on how well done you like your steaks.

Transfer the steaks to serving plates and remove the toothpicks. Serve the steaks with salad greens and cherry tomatoes.

easy but elegant, this dish is great for entertaining

tabasco steaks
with watercress butter

serves 4

1 bunch of watercress
3 oz/85 g unsalted butter,
  softened
4 porterhouse steaks,
  about 8 oz/225 g each
4 tsp Tabasco sauce
salt and pepper

Preheat the barbecue. Using a sharp knife, finely chop enough watercress to fill 4 tablespoons. Reserve a few watercress leaves for the garnish. Place the butter in a small bowl and beat in the chopped watercress with a fork until fully incorporated. Cover with plastic wrap and leave to chill in the refrigerator until required.Sprinkle each steak with 1 teaspoon of the Tabasco sauce, rubbing it in well. Season to taste with salt and pepper.

Cook the steaks over hot coals for 2½ minutes each side for rare, 4 minutes each side for medium, and 6 minutes each side for well done. Transfer to serving plates, garnish with the reserved watercress leaves, and serve immediately, topped with the watercress butter.

this dish brings a touch of class to any party

rack
& ruin

serves 4

4 racks of lamb, each with
  4 chops
2 tbsp extra-virgin olive oil
1 tbsp balsamic vinegar
1 tbsp lemon juice
3 tbsp finely chopped
  fresh rosemary
1 small onion, finely
  chopped
salt and pepper

Place the racks of lamb in a large, shallow, nonmetallic dish. Place the oil, vinegar, lemon juice, rosemary, and onion in a measuring cup and stir together. Season to taste with salt and pepper.

Pour the marinade over the lamb and turn until thoroughly coated. Cover with plastic wrap and let marinate in the refrigerator for 1 hour, turning occasionally.

Preheat the barbecue. Drain the racks of lamb, reserving the marinade. Cook over medium hot coals, brushing frequently with the marinade, for 10 minutes on each side. Serve immediately.

butterflied lamb
with balsamic vinegar & mint

· ·

serves 4

1 boned leg of lamb,
  about 4 lb/1.8 kg
scant ½ cup balsamic
  vinegar
grated rind and juice
  of 1 lemon
⅔ cup corn oil
4 tbsp chopped fresh mint
2 garlic cloves, crushed
2 tbsp brown sugar
salt and pepper

to serve

grilled vegetables, such
  as bell peppers and
  zucchini
black or green olives

Open out the boned leg of lamb so that its shape resembles a butterfly. Thread 2–3 skewers through the meat to make it easier to turn on the grill.

Mix the balsamic vinegar, lemon rind and juice, corn oil, mint, garlic, sugar, and salt and pepper to taste together in a nonmetallic dish that is large enough to hold the lamb. Place the lamb in the dish and turn it over a few times so that the meat is coated on both sides with the marinade. Cover and let marinate in the refrigerator for at least 6 hours, or preferably overnight, turning occasionally.

Preheat the barbecue. Remove the lamb from the marinade and reserve the liquid for basting. Place the rack about 6 inches/ 15 cm above the coals and cook the lamb for 30 minutes on each side, turning once and basting frequently with the marinade.

Transfer the lamb to a cutting board and remove the skewers. Cut the lamb into slices across the grain and serve with grilled vegetables and olives.

a classic combination of herb and citrus flavors

lemon & herb
pork scallops

serves 4

4 pork scallops
2 tbsp corn oil
6 bay leaves, torn into
    pieces
grated rind and juice
    of 2 lemons
½ cup beer
1 tbsp honey
6 juniper berries, lightly
    crushed
salt and pepper
1 crisp apple

Place the pork scallops in a large, shallow, nonmetallic dish. Heat the oil in a small, heavy-bottom pan. Add the bay leaves and stir-fry for 1 minute. Stir in the lemon rind and juice, beer, honey, and juniper berries, and season to taste with salt and pepper.

Pour the mixture over the pork, turning to coat. Cover with plastic wrap, let cool, then let marinate in the refrigerator for up to 8 hours.

Preheat the barbecue. Drain the pork, reserving the marinade. Core the apple and cut into rings. Cook the pork over medium hot coals, brushing frequently with the reserved marinade, for 5 minutes on each side, or until thoroughly cooked. Cook the apples on the barbecue, brushing frequently with the marinade, for 3 minutes. Transfer the pork to a large serving plate with the apple rings and serve immediately.

pork with a medley of tropical fruit and spice

caribbean pork

serves 4

4 pork loin chops
4 tbsp dark brown sugar
4 tbsp orange or pineapple
   juice
2 tbsp Jamaican rum
1 tbsp dry unsweetened
   coconut
½ tsp ground cinnamon
mixed salad greens,
   to serve

coconut rice
generous 1 cup basmati
   rice
2 cups water
⅔ cup coconut milk
4 tbsp raisins
4 tbsp roasted peanuts or
   cashews
salt and pepper
2 tbsp dry unsweetened
   coconut, toasted

Trim any excess fat from the pork and place the chops in a shallow, nonmetallic dish. Mix the sugar, fruit juice, rum, coconut, and cinnamon together in a bowl, stirring until the sugar dissolves. Pour the mixture over the pork, cover, and let marinate in the refrigerator for 2 hours, or preferably overnight.

Preheat the barbecue. Remove the pork from the marinade, reserving the liquid for basting. Cook over hot coals for 15–20 minutes, basting with the marinade.

Meanwhile, make the coconut rice. Rinse the rice under cold running water, place it in a pan with the water and coconut milk, and bring gently to a boil. Stir, cover, and reduce the heat. Simmer gently for 12 minutes, or until the rice is tender and the liquid has been absorbed. Fluff up with a fork.

Stir the raisins and nuts into the rice, season to taste with salt and pepper, and sprinkle with the dry unsweetened coconut. Transfer the pork and rice to warmed serving plates and serve immediately with mixed salad greens.

these golden spicy poussins are sure to impress

butterflied
poussins

serves 4

4 poussins, about
    1 lb/450 g each
1 tbsp paprika
1 tbsp mustard powder
1 tbsp ground cumin
pinch of cayenne pepper
1 tbsp ketchup
1 tbsp lemon juice
salt
5 tbsp melted butter
fresh cilantro sprigs,
    to garnish
corn on the cob, to serve

To butterfly the poussins, turn 1 bird breast-side down and, using strong kitchen scissors or poultry shears, cut through the skin and rib cage along both sides of the backbone, from tail to neck. Remove the backbone and turn the bird breast-side up. Press down firmly on the breastbone to flatten. Fold the wingtips underneath. Push a skewer through one wing, the top of the breast, and out of the other wing. Push a second skewer through one thigh, the bottom of the breast, and out through the other thigh. Repeat with the remaining poussins.

Mix the paprika, mustard powder, cumin, cayenne, ketchup, and lemon juice together in a small bowl and season to taste with salt. Gradually stir in the butter to make a smooth paste. Spread the paste evenly over the poussins, cover, and let marinate in the refrigerator for up to 8 hours.

Preheat the barbecue. Cook the poussins over medium hot coals, turning frequently, for 25–30 minutes, brushing with a little oil if necessary. Transfer to a serving plate, garnish with fresh cilantro sprigs, and serve with corn on the cob.

tarragon and turkey form an ideal partnership

tarragon turkey

serves 4

4 turkey breasts, about
  6 oz/175 g each
salt and pepper
4 tsp whole-grain mustard
8 fresh tarragon sprigs,
  plus extra to garnish
4 smoked Canadian bacon
  strips
salad greens, to serve

Preheat the barbecue. Season the turkey to taste with salt and pepper, and, using a round-bladed knife, spread the mustard evenly over the turkey.

Place 2 tarragon sprigs on top of each turkey breast and wrap a bacon strip around it to hold the herbs in place. Secure with a toothpick.

Cook the turkey over medium hot coals for 5–8 minutes on each side. Transfer to serving plates and garnish with tarragon sprigs. Serve with salad greens.

apricots are the perfect foil to the rich duck

fruity duck

serves 4

4 duck breasts
⅔ cup dried apricots
2 shallots, thinly sliced
2 tbsp honey
1 tsp sesame oil
2 tsp Chinese five-spice
  powder

Preheat the barbecue. Using a sharp knife, cut a long slit in the fleshy side of each duck breast to make a pocket. Divide the apricots and shallots among the pockets and secure with skewers.

Mix the honey and sesame oil together in a small bowl and brush all over the duck. Sprinkle with the Chinese five-spice powder.

Cook the duck over medium hot coals for 6–8 minutes on each side. Remove the skewers, transfer to a large serving plate, and serve immediately.

meaty and succulent monkfish is great for the barbecue

orange & lemon peppered monkfish

∙∙

serves 8

2 oranges
2 lemons
2 monkfish tails, about
    1 lb 2 oz/500 g each,
    skinned and cut into
    4 fillets
8 fresh lemon thyme
    sprigs
2 tbsp olive oil
salt
2 tbsp green peppercorns,
    lightly crushed

Cut 8 orange slices and 8 lemon slices, reserving the remaining fruit. Rinse the monkfish fillets under cold running water and pat dry with paper towels. Place the monkfish fillets, cut side up, on a counter and divide the citrus slices among them. Top with the lemon thyme. Tie each fillet at intervals with kitchen string to secure the citrus slices and thyme. Place the monkfish in a large, shallow, nonmetallic dish.

Squeeze the juice from the remaining fruit and mix with the olive oil in a measuring cup. Season to taste with salt, then spoon the mixture over the fish. Cover with plastic wrap and let marinate in the refrigerator for up to 1 hour, spooning the marinade over the fish tails once or twice.

Preheat the barbecue. Drain the monkfish tails, reserving the marinade. Sprinkle the crushed green peppercorns over the fish, pressing them in with your fingers. Cook the monkfish over medium hot coals, turning and brushing frequently with the reserved marinade, for 20–25 minutes. Transfer to a cutting board, remove and discard the string, and cut the monkfish tails into slices. Serve immediately.

an extra-special fish dish with Indonesian spices

grilled red snapper

serves 4

4 banana leaves
2 limes
3 garlic cloves
4 red snappers, about
  12 oz/350 g each
2 scallions, thinly sliced
1-inch/2.5-cm piece fresh
  gingerroot
1 onion, finely chopped
4½ tsp peanut or corn oil
3 tbsp kecap manis or
  light soy sauce
1 tsp ground coriander
1 tsp ground cumin
¼ tsp ground cloves
¼ tsp ground turmeric

Preheat the barbecue. If necessary, cut the banana leaves into 4 x 16-inch/40-cm squares, using a sharp knife or scissors. Thinly slice 1½ limes and 1 garlic clove. Clean and scale the fish, then rinse it inside and out under cold running water. Pat dry with paper towels. Using a sharp knife, make a series of deep diagonal slashes on the side of each fish, then insert the lime and garlic slices into the slashes. Place the fish on the banana leaf squares and sprinkle with the scallions.

Finely chop the remaining garlic and squeeze the juice from the remaining lime half. Finely chop the ginger, then place the garlic in a bowl with the onion, ginger, oil, kecap manis, spices, and lime juice, and mix to a paste.

Spoon the paste into the fish cavities and spread it over the outside. Roll up the packages and tie securely with string. Cook over medium hot coals, turning occasionally, for 15–20 minutes. Serve.

these succulent shrimp will be loved by all

shrimp
with citrus salsa

serves 6

36 large, raw jumbo
   shrimp
2 tbsp finely chopped fresh
   cilantro
pinch of cayenne pepper
3–4 tbsp corn oil
fresh cilantro leaves, to
   garnish
lime wedges, to serve

salsa
1 orange
1 tart apple, peeled,
   quartered, and cored
2 fresh red chiles,
   seeded and chopped
1 garlic clove, chopped
8 fresh cilantro sprigs
8 fresh mint sprigs
4 tbsp lime juice
salt and pepper

Preheat the barbecue. To make the salsa, peel the orange and cut into segments. Set aside any juice. Put the orange segments, apple quarters, chiles, garlic, cilantro, and mint into a food processor and process until smooth. With the motor running, add the lime juice through the feeder tube. Transfer the salsa to a serving bowl and season to taste with salt and pepper. Cover with plastic wrap and let chill in the refrigerator until required.

Using a sharp knife, remove and discard the heads from the shrimp, then remove the shells. Cut along the back of the shrimp and remove the dark intestinal vein. Rinse the shrimp under cold running water and pat dry with paper towels. Mix the chopped cilantro, cayenne, and corn oil together in a dish. Add the shrimp and toss well to coat.

Cook the shrimp over medium hot coals for 3 minutes on each side, or until they have changed color. Transfer to a large serving plate, garnish with fresh cilantro leaves, and serve immediately with lime wedges and the salsa.

this dish is simple to prepare and tastes delicious

stuffed sardines

serves 6

1 tbsp fresh parsley,
  finely chopped
4 garlic cloves, finely
  chopped
12 fresh sardines, cleaned
  and scaled
3 tbsp lemon juice
scant ⅔ cup all-purpose
  flour
1 tsp ground cumin
salt and pepper
olive oil, for brushing

Place the parsley and garlic in a bowl and mix together. Rinse the fish inside and out under cold running water and pat dry with paper towels. Spoon the herb mixture into the fish cavities and pat the remainder all over the outside of the fish. Sprinkle the sardines with lemon juice and transfer to a large, shallow, nonmetallic dish. Cover with plastic wrap and let marinate in the refrigerator for 1 hour.

Preheat the barbecue. Mix the flour and ground cumin together in a bowl, then season to taste with salt and pepper. Spread out the seasoned flour on a large plate and gently roll the sardines in the flour to coat.

Brush the sardines with olive oil and cook over medium hot coals for 3–4 minutes on each side. Serve immediately.

oysters and bacon make an appetizing delicacy

charbroiled
devils

. . . .

serves 6

36 fresh oysters
18 rindless lean bacon
    strips
1 tbsp mild paprika
1 tsp cayenne pepper

sauce
1 fresh red chile, seeded
    and finely chopped
1 garlic clove, finely
    chopped
1 shallot, finely chopped
2 tbsp finely chopped fresh
    parsley
2 tbsp lemon juice
salt and pepper

Preheat the barbecue. Open the oysters, catching the juice from the shells in a bowl. Cut the oysters from the bottom shells, set aside, and tip any remaining juice into the bowl. To make the sauce, add the red chile, garlic, shallot, parsley, and lemon juice to the bowl, then season to taste with salt and pepper and mix well. Cover the bowl with plastic wrap and let chill in the refrigerator until required.

Using a sharp knife, cut each bacon strip in half across the center. Season the oysters with paprika and cayenne, then roll each oyster up inside half a bacon strip. Thread 6 wrapped oysters onto each presoaked wooden skewer.

Cook over hot coals, turning frequently, for 5 minutes, or until the bacon is well browned and crispy. Transfer to a large serving plate and serve immediately with the sauce.

you can vary the filling of these tasty mushrooms

stuffed mushrooms

serves 12

12 portobello mushrooms
4 tsp olive oil
4 scallions, chopped
2 cups fresh brown
   breadcrumbs
1 tsp chopped fresh
   oregano
3½ oz/100 g feta cheese or
   chorizo sausage
corn oil, for oiling

Preheat the barbecue. Remove the stems from the mushrooms and chop the stems finely. Heat half of the olive oil in a large skillet. Add the mushroom stems and scallions and cook briefly.

Mix the mushroom stems and scallions together in a large bowl. Add the breadcrumbs and oregano to the mushrooms and scallions, mix well, then reserve until required.

If using feta, crumble the cheese into small pieces in a small bowl. If you are using chorizo sausage, remove the skin and chop the flesh finely.

Add the crumbled feta cheese or chopped chorizo to the breadcrumb mixture and mix well. Spoon the stuffing mixture into the mushroom caps.

Drizzle the remaining olive oil over the stuffed mushrooms, then cook on an oiled rack over medium hot coals for 8–10 minutes. Transfer the mushrooms to individual serving plates and serve while still hot.

zucchini and feta are a stunning combination

zucchini & cheese packages

serves 2

1 small bunch of
   fresh mint
2 large zucchini
1 tbsp olive oil, plus extra
   for brushing
4 oz/115 g feta cheese,
   cut into strips
pepper

Preheat the barbecue. Using a sharp knife, finely chop enough mint to fill 1 tablespoon. Set aside until required. Cut out 2 rectangles of foil, each large enough to enclose a zucchini, and brush lightly with olive oil. Cut a few slits along the length of each zucchini and place them on the foil rectangles.

Insert strips of feta cheese along the slits in the zucchini, then drizzle the olive oil over the top, sprinkle with the reserved chopped mint, and season to taste with pepper. Fold in the sides of the foil rectangles securely and seal the edges to enclose the cheese-filled zucchini completely.

Bake the packages in the barbecue embers for 30–40 minutes. Carefully unwrap the packages and serve immediately.

stuffed tomato
packages

serves 4

1 tbsp olive oil
2 tbsp sunflower seeds
1 onion, finely chopped
1 garlic clove, finely
   chopped
1 lb 2 oz/500 g fresh
   spinach, thick stalks
   removed and leaves
   shredded
pinch of freshly grated
   nutmeg
salt and pepper
4 beefsteak tomatoes
5 oz/140 g mozzarella
   cheese, diced

Preheat the barbecue. Heat the oil in a heavy-bottom pan. Add the sunflower seeds and cook, stirring constantly, for 2 minutes, or until golden. Add the onion and cook over low heat, stirring occasionally, for 5 minutes, or until softened but not browned. Add the garlic and spinach, cover, and cook for 2–3 minutes, or until the spinach has wilted. Remove the pan from the heat and season to taste with nutmeg, salt, and pepper. Let cool.

Using a sharp knife, cut off and set aside a thin slice from the top of each tomato and scoop out the flesh with a teaspoon, taking care not to pierce the shell. Chop the flesh and stir it into the spinach mixture with the mozzarella cheese.

Fill the tomato shells with the spinach and cheese mixture and replace the tops. Cut 4 squares of foil, each large enough to enclose a tomato. Place one tomato in the center of each square and fold up the sides to enclose securely. Cook over hot coals, turning occasionally, for 10 minutes. Serve immediately in the foil packages.

Burgers

this homemade burger is the ultimate barbecue treat

the classic
hamburger

· ·

serves 4–6

1 lb/450 g sirloin or top
  round, freshly ground
1 onion, grated
2–4 garlic cloves, crushed
2 tsp whole-grain mustard
pepper
2 tbsp olive oil
1 lb/450 g onions, finely
  sliced
2 tsp brown sugar
hamburger buns, to serve

Place the ground beef, onion, garlic, mustard, and pepper in a large bowl and mix together. Shape into 4–6 equal-size burgers, then cover and let chill for 30 minutes.

Meanwhile, heat the oil in a heavy-bottom skillet. Add the onions and sauté over low heat for 10–15 minutes, or until the onions have caramelized. Add the sugar after 8 minutes and stir occasionally during cooking. Drain well on paper towels and keep warm.

Preheat the barbecue. Cook the burgers over hot coals for 3–5 minutes on each side or until cooked to personal preference. Serve in hamburger buns with the onions.

beef burgers with chile & basil

· ·

serves 4

1 lb 7 oz/650 g ground beef
1 red bell pepper, seeded
  and finely chopped
1 garlic clove, finely
  chopped
2 small red chiles, seeded
  and finely chopped
1 tbsp chopped fresh basil
½ tsp ground cumin
salt and pepper
sprigs of fresh basil,
  to garnish
hamburger buns, to serve

Put the ground beef, red bell pepper, garlic, chiles, chopped basil, and cumin into a bowl and mix until well combined. Season with salt and pepper. Using your hands, form the mixture into burger shapes.

Preheat the barbecue. Cook the burgers over hot coals for 5–8 minutes on each side, or until cooked through. Garnish with sprigs of basil and serve in hamburger buns.

pork burgers
with tangy orange marinade

serves 4–6

1 lb/450 g pork fillet,
  cut into small pieces
3 tbsp Seville orange
  marmalade
2 tbsp orange juice
1 tbsp balsamic vinegar
8 oz/225 g parsnips,
  cut into chunks
1 tbsp finely grated
  orange rind
2 garlic cloves, crushed
6 scallions, finely chopped
1 zucchini (6 oz/175 g),
  grated
salt and pepper
1 tbsp corn oil
lettuce leaves, to serve
hamburger buns, to serve

Place the pork in a shallow dish. Place the marmalade, orange juice, and vinegar in a small pan and heat, stirring, until the marmalade has melted. Pour the marinade over the pork. Cover and let stand for at least 30 minutes, or longer if time permits. Remove the pork, reserving the marinade. Grind the pork into a large bowl.

Meanwhile, cook the parsnips in a pan of boiling water for 15–20 minutes, or until cooked. Drain, then mash and add to the pork. Stir in the orange rind, garlic, scallions, zucchini, and salt and pepper to taste. Mix together, then shape into 4–6 equal-size burgers. Cover and let chill for at least 30 minutes.

Preheat the barbecue. When hot, lightly brush the burgers with oil and cook over hot coals for 4–6 minutes on each side or until thoroughly cooked. Boil the reserved marinade for at least 5 minutes, then pour into a small pitcher or bowl. Serve with the lettuce leaves in hamburger buns.

cajun spices give this burger a
fabulous smoky tang

barbecued
cajun pork burgers

serves 4–6

8 oz/225 g sweet potatoes,
  cut into chunks
salt and pepper
1 lb/450 g fresh ground
  pork
1 Granny Smith or other
  apple, peeled, cored, and
  grated
2 tsp Cajun seasoning
1 lb/450 g onions
1 tbsp chopped fresh
  cilantro
2 tbsp corn oil
8–12 lean Canadian bacon
  slices

Cook the sweet potato in a pan of lightly salted boiling water for 15–20 minutes, or until soft when pierced with a fork. Drain well, then mash and set aside.

Place the ground pork in a bowl, add the mashed potato, grated apple, and Cajun seasoning. Grate 1 of the onions and add to the pork mixture with salt and pepper to taste and the chopped cilantro. Mix together, then shape into 4–6 equal-size burgers. Cover and let chill for 1 hour.

Preheat the barbecue. Slice the remaining onions. Heat 1 tablespoon of the oil in a skillet. Add the onions and cook over low heat for 10–12 minutes, stirring until soft. Remove the skillet from the heat and set aside. Wrap each burger in 2 slices of bacon.

Cook the burgers over hot coals, brushing with the remaining oil for 4–5 minutes on each side, or until thoroughly cooked. Serve with the fried onions.

lamb and fresh mint are a classic
partnership

minty lamb
burgers

∙∙

serves 4–6

1 red bell pepper, seeded
    and cut into quarters
1 yellow bell pepper, seeded
    and cut into quarters
1 red onion, cut into thick
    wedges
1 baby eggplant (4 oz/
    115 g), cut into wedges
2 tbsp olive oil
1 lb/450 g fresh ground
    lamb
2 tbsp freshly grated
    Parmesan cheese
1 tbsp chopped fresh mint
salt and pepper

**minty mustard
mayonnaise**
4 tbsp mayonnaise
1 tsp Dijon mustard
1 tbsp chopped fresh mint

to serve
hamburger buns
shredded lettuce
grilled vegetables,
    such as bell peppers and
    cherry tomatoes

Preheat the broiler to medium. Place the bell peppers, onion,
and eggplant on a foil-lined broiler rack, brush the eggplant with
1 tablespoon of the oil, and cook under the hot broiler for 10–12
minutes, or until charred. Remove from the broiler, let cool, then
peel the bell peppers. Place all the vegetables in a food processor
and, using the pulse button, chop.

Add the ground lamb, Parmesan cheese, chopped mint, and salt
and pepper to the food processor and blend until the mixture
comes together. Scrape onto a board and shape into 4–6 equal-
size burgers. Cover and let chill for at least 30 minutes.

To make the minty mustard mayonnaise, blend the mayonnaise
with the mustard and chopped fresh mint. Cover and chill
until required.

Preheat the barbecue. Lightly brush the burgers with the
remaining oil, and cook over hot coals for 3–4 minutes on each
side or until cooked to personal preference. Serve the burgers
in hamburger buns with the shredded lettuce and prepared
mayonnaise, and a selection of grilled vegetables on the side.

lamb & feta
burgers

serves 4–6

1 lb/450 g fresh ground lamb
8 oz/225 g feta cheese, crumbled
2 garlic cloves, crushed
6 scallions, finely chopped
½ cup prunes, chopped
2 tbsp pine nuts, toasted
1 cup fresh whole-wheat breadcrumbs
1 tbsp chopped fresh rosemary
salt and pepper
1 tbsp corn oil

Place the ground lamb in a large bowl with the feta, garlic, scallions, prunes, pine nuts, and breadcrumbs. Mix well, breaking up any lumps of meat.

Add the rosemary and salt and pepper to the lamb mixture in the bowl. Mix together, then shape into 4–6 equal-size burgers. Cover and let chill for 30 minutes.

Preheat the barbecue. Brush the burgers lightly with oil and cook over hot coals for 4 minutes before turning over and brushing with the remaining oil. Continue to cook for 4 minutes, or until cooked to personal preference. Serve.

these breaded chicken burgers are deliciously tender

the ultimate
chicken burger

· ·

serves 4

4 large chicken breast
  fillets, skinned
1 large egg white
1 tbsp cornstarch
1 tbsp all-purpose flour
1 egg, beaten
1 cup fresh white
  breadcrumbs
2 tbsp corn oil
2 beefsteak tomatoes,
  sliced

to serve
hamburger buns
shredded lettuce
mayonnaise

Place the chicken breasts between 2 sheets of nonstick parchment paper and flatten slightly using a meat mallet or a rolling pin. Beat the egg white and cornstarch together, then brush over the chicken. Cover and let chill for 30 minutes, then coat in the flour.

Place the egg and breadcrumbs in 2 separate bowls and coat the burgers first in the egg, allowing any excess to drip back into the bowl, then in the breadcrumbs.

Preheat the barbecue. When hot, add the burgers and cook over hot coals for 6–8 minutes on each side, or until thoroughly cooked. If you are in doubt, it is worth cutting one of the burgers in half. If there is any sign of pinkness, cook for a little longer. Add the tomato slices for the last 1–2 minutes of the cooking time to heat through. Serve the burgers in hamburger buns with the shredded lettuce, cooked tomato slices, and mayonnaise.

maple-glazed
turkey burgers

serves 4

2 fresh corn cobs with
    husks intact
1 lb/450 g fresh ground
    turkey
1 red bell pepper, seeded,
    peeled, and finely
    chopped
6 scallions, finely chopped
1 cup fresh white
    breadcrumbs
2 tbsp chopped fresh basil
salt and pepper
1 tbsp corn oil
2 tbsp maple syrup

to serve
hamburger buns
salad greens
tomato slices

Heat a grill pan until hot, then add the fresh corn cobs and cook over medium-high heat for 8–10 minutes, turning every 2–3 minutes, or until the husks are charred. Remove from the grill pan, let cool, then strip off the husks and silk. Using a sharp knife, cut away the kernels and place in a bowl.

Add the ground turkey, red bell pepper, scallions, breadcrumbs, basil, salt, and pepper to the corn kernels in the bowl. Mix together, then shape into 4 equal-size burgers. Cover and let chill for 1 hour.

Preheat the barbecue. Brush the burgers lightly with oil, glaze with half of the maple syrup and cook over hot coals for 4 minutes. Turn over the burgers and brush with the remaining oil and maple syrup and continue to cook for 4 minutes, or until cooked to personal preference. Serve the burgers in hamburger buns with the salad greens and tomato slices.

an inspiring variation on the traditional fish cake

fish burgers

· ·

serves 4

5 oz/140 g potatoes,
    cut into chunks
salt and pepper
8 oz/225 g cod fillet,
    skinned
8 oz/225 g haddock,
    skinned
1 tbsp grated lemon rind
1 tbsp chopped fresh
    parsley
1–2 tbsp all-purpose flour
1 egg, beaten
1½ cups fresh white
    breadcrumbs
2 tbsp corn oil
hamburger buns, to serve

Cook the potatoes in a pan of lightly salted boiling water for 15–20 minutes, or until tender. Drain well and mash. Chop the fish into small pieces, then place in a food processor with the mashed potatoes, lemon rind, parsley, and salt and pepper to taste. Using the pulse button, blend together. Shape into 4 equal-size burgers and coat in the flour. Cover and let chill for 30 minutes.

Place the egg and breadcrumbs in 2 separate bowls and coat the burgers first in the egg, allowing any excess to drip back into the bowl, then in the breadcrumbs. Let chill for an additional 30 minutes.

Preheat the barbecue. Brush the burgers lightly with oil and cook over hot coals for 4–5 minutes on each side, or until golden and cooked through. Serve in toasted hamburger buns.

tuna is an excellent choice for the barbecue

tuna burgers
with mango salsa

serves 4–6

8 oz/225 g sweet potatoes, chopped
salt
1 lb/450 g fresh tuna steaks
6 scallions, finely chopped
6 oz/175 g zucchini, grated
1 fresh red jalapeño chile, seeded and finely chopped
2 tbsp prepared mango chutney
1 tbsp corn oil
lettuce leaves, to serve

mango salsa

1 large ripe mango, peeled and seeded
2 ripe tomatoes, finely chopped
1 fresh red jalapeño chile, seeded and finely chopped
1½-inch/4-cm piece cucumber, finely diced
1 tbsp chopped fresh cilantro
1–2 tsp honey

Cook the sweet potatoes in a pan of lightly salted boiling water for 15–20 minutes, or until tender. Drain well, then mash and place in a food processor. Cut the tuna into chunks and add to the potatoes.

Add the scallions, zucchini, chile, and mango chutney to the food processor and, using the pulse button, blend together. Shape into 4–6 equal-size burgers, then cover and let chill for 1 hour.

Meanwhile, make the salsa. Slice the mango flesh, reserving 8–12 good slices for serving. Finely chop the remainder, then mix with the tomatoes, chile, cucumber, cilantro, and honey. Mix well, then spoon into a small bowl. Cover and let stand for 30 minutes to allow the flavors to develop.

Preheat the barbecue. Brush the burgers lightly with oil and cook over hot coals for 4–6 minutes on each side, or until piping hot. Serve with the mango salsa, garnished with lettuce leaves and the reserved slices of mango.

a winning combination of rice, beans, and nuts

the ultimate
vegetarian burger

serves 4–6

scant ½ cup brown rice
salt and pepper
14 oz/400 g canned
    flageolets, drained
scant 1 cup unsalted
    cashews
3 garlic cloves
1 red onion, cut into
    wedges
½ cup corn kernels
2 tbsp tomato paste
1 tbsp chopped fresh
    oregano
2 tbsp whole wheat flour
2 tbsp corn oil

to serve
hamburger buns
lettuce leaves
tomato slices
cheese slices

Cook the rice in a pan of lightly salted boiling water for 20 minutes, or until tender. Drain and place in a food processor.

Add the beans, cashews, garlic, onion, corn, tomato paste, oregano, and salt and pepper to the rice in the food processor and, using the pulse button, blend together. Shape into 4–6 equal-size burgers, then coat in the flour. Cover and let chill for 1 hour.

Preheat the barbecue. Brush the burgers lightly with oil and cook over hot coals for 5–6 minutes on each side or until cooked and piping hot. Serve the burgers in hamburger buns with the lettuce leaves, and tomato and cheese slices.

three-bean burgers
with green mayo

serves 4–6

10½ oz/300 g canned
   cannellini beans, drained
10½ oz/300 g canned
   black-eyed peas, drained
10½ oz/300 g canned red
   kidney beans, drained
   and rinsed
1 fresh red chile, deseeded
4 shallots, cut into
   quarters
2 celery stalks, coarsely
   chopped
1 cup fresh whole wheat
   breadcrumbs
1 tbsp chopped fresh
   cilantro
salt and pepper
2 tbsp whole wheat flour
2 tbsp corn oil
hamburger buns, to serve

green mayo
6 tbsp prepared
   mayonnaise
2 tbsp chopped fresh
   parsley or mint
1 tbsp chopped cucumber
3 scallions, finely chopped

Place the beans, chile, shallots, celery, breadcrumbs, cilantro, and salt and pepper in a food processor and, using the pulse button, blend together. Shape into 4–6 equal-size burgers, then cover and let chill for 1 hour. Coat the burgers lightly in the flour.

To make the green mayo, place the mayonnaise, parsley, cucumber, and scallions in a bowl and mix together. Cover and chill until required.

Preheat the barbecue. Brush the burgers lightly with oil and cook over hot coals for 5–6 minutes on each side, or until piping hot. Serve in hamburger buns with the green mayo.

these burgers may be lacking in meat but not in flavor

mushroom
burgers

· ·

serves 4

4 oz/115 g button
   mushrooms
1 carrot
1 onion
1 zucchini
2 tsp corn oil, plus extra
   for brushing
¼ cup peanuts
2 cups fresh white
   breadcrumbs
1 tbsp chopped fresh
   parsley
1 tsp yeast extract
salt and pepper
1 tbsp all-purpose flour,
   for dusting

Using a sharp knife, finely chop the mushrooms, then chop the carrot, onion, and zucchini, and set aside. Heat the oil in a heavy-bottom skillet, add the mushrooms, and cook, stirring, for 8 minutes, or until all the moisture has evaporated. Using a slotted spoon, transfer the cooked mushrooms to a large bowl.

Put the carrot, onion, zucchini, and peanuts into a food processor and process until finely chopped. Transfer to the bowl containing the mushrooms and stir in the breadcrumbs, chopped parsley, and yeast extract. Season to taste with salt and pepper. Lightly flour your hands and form the mixture into 4 patties. Place on a large plate, cover with plastic wrap, and let chill in the refrigerator for at least 1 hour and up to 1 day.

Preheat the barbecue. Brush the mushroom burgers with the corn oil and cook over hot coals for 8–10 minutes. Serve.

Skewers

this is a barbecue version of the classic dish

surf 'n' turf

skewers

• •

serves 2

8 oz/225 g beef tenderloin,
about 1 inch/
2.5 cm thick
8 raw jumbo shrimp,
in their shells
olive oil, for oiling
salt and pepper
4 tbsp butter
2 garlic cloves, crushed
3 tbsp chopped fresh
parsley, plus extra
parsley sprigs,
to garnish
finely grated rind and
juice of 1 lime
lime wedges, to garnish
crusty bread, to serve

Cut the steak into 1 inch/2.5 cm cubes. To prepare the shrimp, pull off their heads with your fingers, then peel off their shells, leaving the tails on. Using a sharp knife, make a shallow slit along the underside of each shrimp, then pull out the dark vein and discard. Rinse the shrimp under cold running water and dry well on paper towels.

Thread an equal number of the steak cubes and shrimp onto 2 oiled metal kabob skewers or presoaked wooden skewers. Season the kabobs to taste with pepper.

Preheat the barbecue. Meanwhile, put the butter and garlic into a small pan and heat gently until melted. Remove from the heat and add the parsley, lime rind and juice, and salt and pepper to taste. Leave in a warm place so that the butter remains melted.

Brush the kabobs with a little of the melted butter. Put the kabobs onto an oiled grill rack and cook over medium heat for 4–8 minutes until the steak is cooked according to your taste and the shrimp turn pink, turning the kabobs frequently during cooking, and brushing with the remaining melted butter.

Serve the kabobs hot on the skewers, with the remaining butter spooned over. Garnish with lime wedges and parsley sprigs and serve with crusty bread to mop up the buttery juices.

beef in a classic japanese-style marinade

beef **teriyaki**

•••

serves 4

1 lb/450 g extra-thin beef
  steaks
1 yellow bell pepper,
  seeded and cut into
  chunks
8 scallions, trimmed and
  cut into short lengths
salad greens, to serve

sauce

1 tsp cornstarch
2 tbsp dry sherry
2 tbsp white wine vinegar
3 tbsp soy sauce
1 tbsp dark brown sugar
1 garlic clove, crushed
½ tsp ground cinnamon
½ tsp ground ginger

Place the beef steaks in a shallow, nonmetallic dish. To make the sauce, mix the cornstarch and sherry together in a small bowl, then stir in the remaining sauce ingredients. Pour the sauce over the meat, cover with plastic wrap, and let marinate in the refrigerator for at least 2 hours.

Preheat the barbecue. Remove the meat from the sauce and reserve. Pour the sauce into a small pan and cook for at least 5 minutes, stirring occasionally.

Cut the meat into thin strips and thread these, concertina-style, onto several presoaked wooden skewers, alternating each strip of meat with the pieces of bell pepper and scallion. Cook the kabobs over hot coals for 5–8 minutes, turning and basting the beef and vegetables occasionally with the reserved sauce.

Arrange the skewers on serving plates, pour over the remaining sauce, and serve with salad greens.

spicy meat patties molded around kabob skewers

indian kofta

• •

serves 4

1 small onion
1 lb/450 g fresh lean
 ground lamb
2 tbsp curry paste
2 tbsp plain yogurt
corn oil, for basting

tomato sambal
3 tomatoes, seeded
 and diced
pinch of ground coriander
pinch of ground cumin
2 tsp chopped fresh
 cilantro
salt and pepper

to serve
pappadams
chutney

Place the onion in a food processor and chop finely. Add the lamb and process briefly to chop further. Chopping the meat again will help the kofta mixture to hold together during cooking. Alternatively, grate the onion finely before mixing it with the lamb.

Add the curry paste and yogurt and mix well. Divide the mixture into 8 equal-size portions. Press and shape the mixture into 8 sausage shapes and push each one onto a metal or presoaked wooden skewer, pressing the mixture together firmly so that it holds its shape. Let chill in the refrigerator for at least 30 minutes, or until required.

To make the tomato sambal, mix the tomatoes, spices, chopped cilantro, and salt and pepper to taste together in a bowl. Let stand for at least 30 minutes for the flavors to combine.

Preheat the barbecue. Cook the kabobs on an oiled rack over hot coals for 10–15 minutes, turning frequently. Baste with a little corn oil if needed. Serve accompanied with pappadams, chutney, and tomato sambal.

these fragrant kabobs are a georgian speciality

shashlik

· ·

serves 4

1 lb 8 oz/675 g boneless
  leg of lamb, cut into
  1-inch/2.5-cm cubes
12 button mushrooms
4 rindless lean bacon
  strips
8 cherry tomatoes
1 large green bell pepper,
  seeded and cut into
  squares
crusty bread, to serve

marinade
4 tbsp corn oil
4 tbsp lemon juice
1 onion, finely chopped
½ tsp dried rosemary
½ tsp dried thyme
salt and pepper

Place the lamb and mushrooms in a large, shallow, nonmetallic dish. Mix all the ingredients for the marinade together in a measuring cup, seasoning to taste with salt and pepper. Pour the mixture over the lamb and mushrooms, turning to coat. Cover with plastic wrap and let marinate in the refrigerator for up to 8 hours.

Preheat the barbecue. Cut the bacon strips in half across the center and stretch with a heavy, flat-bladed knife, then roll up. Drain the lamb and mushrooms, reserving the marinade. Thread the bacon rolls, lamb, mushrooms, tomatoes, and bell pepper squares alternately onto metal skewers. Strain the marinade.

Cook the kabobs over medium hot coals, turning and brushing frequently with the reserved marinade, for 10–15 minutes. Transfer to a large serving plate and serve immediately with crusty bread.

a classic combination of pork and apple

pork & apple
skewers

••

serves 4

1 lb/450 g pork fillet
1¼ cups hard cider
1 tbsp finely chopped fresh
  sage
6 black peppercorns,
  crushed
2 crisp apples
1 tbsp corn oil
crusty bread, to serve

Using a sharp knife, cut the pork into 1-inch/2.5-cm cubes, then place in a large, shallow, nonmetallic dish. Mix the cider, sage, and peppercorns together in a measuring cup, pour the mixture over the pork and turn until thoroughly coated. Cover and let marinate in the refrigerator for 1–2 hours.

Preheat the barbecue. Drain the pork, reserving the marinade. Core the apples, but do not peel, then cut into wedges. Dip the apple wedges into the reserved marinade and thread onto several metal skewers, alternating with the cubes of pork. Stir the corn oil into the remaining marinade.

Cook the brochettes over medium hot coals, turning and brushing frequently with the reserved marinade, for 12–15 minutes. Transfer to a large serving plate and if you prefer, remove the meat and apples from the skewers before serving. Serve immediately with crusty bread.

these slightly sweet skewers are popular with children

pork & sage
kabobs

● ●

serves 4

1 lb/450 g ground pork
½ cup fresh breadcrumbs
1 small onion, very finely
   chopped
1 tbsp fresh sage, chopped
2 tbsp applesauce
¼ tsp ground nutmeg
salt and pepper

baste
3 tbsp olive oil
1 tbsp lemon juice

to serve
4 small pita breads
mixed salad greens
6 tbsp thick plain yogurt

Place the pork in a mixing bowl, together with the breadcrumbs, onion, sage, applesauce, nutmeg, and salt and pepper to taste. Mix until the ingredients are well combined.

Using your hands, shape the mixture into small balls, about the size of large marbles, and chill in the refrigerator for at least 30 minutes.

Meanwhile, soak several small wooden skewers in cold water for at least 30 minutes. Thread the meatballs onto the skewers.

To make the baste, mix together the oil and lemon juice in a small bowl, whisking with a fork until it is well blended.

Cook the kabobs over hot coals for 8–10 minutes, turning and basting frequently with the lemon and oil mixture, until the meat is golden and cooked through.

Line the pita breads with the salad greens and spoon some of the yogurt on top. Serve with the kabobs.

chicken in a zingy marinade of citrus juice and rind

zesty kabobs

••

serves 4

4 skinless, boneless
  chicken breasts, about
  6 oz/175 g each
finely grated rind and
  juice of ½ lemon
finely grated rind and
  juice of ½ orange
2 tbsp honey
2 tbsp olive oil
2 tbsp chopped fresh mint,
  plus extra to garnish
¼ tsp ground coriander
salt and pepper
citrus zest, to garnish

Using a sharp knife, cut the chicken into 1-inch/2.5-cm cubes, then place them in a large glass bowl. Place the lemon and orange rind, the lemon and orange juice, the honey, oil, mint, and ground coriander in a measuring cup and mix together. Season to taste with salt and pepper. Pour the marinade over the chicken cubes and toss until thoroughly coated. Cover with plastic wrap and let marinate in the refrigerator for up to 8 hours.

Preheat the barbecue. Drain the chicken cubes, reserving the marinade. Thread the chicken onto several long metal skewers.

Cook the skewers over medium hot coals, turning and brushing frequently with the reserved marinade, for 6–10 minutes, or until thoroughly cooked. Transfer to a large serving plate, garnish with fresh chopped mint and citrus zest, and serve immediately.

these chicken skewers are wonderfully aromatic

chicken satay

· ·

serves 4

8 tbsp crunchy peanut
  butter
1 onion, coarsely chopped
1 garlic clove, coarsely
  chopped
2 tbsp creamed coconut
4 tbsp peanut oil
1 tsp light soy sauce
2 tbsp lime juice
2 fresh red chiles, seeded
  and chopped
3 kaffir lime leaves, torn
4 skinless, boneless
  chicken breasts, about
  6 oz/175 g each, cut into
  1-inch/2.5-cm cubes

Put the peanut butter, onion, garlic, coconut, peanut oil, soy sauce, lime juice, chiles, and lime leaves into a food processor and process to a smooth paste. Transfer the paste to a large glass bowl.

Add the chicken cubes to the dish and stir to coat thoroughly. Cover with plastic wrap and let marinate in the refrigerator for up to 8 hours.

Preheat the barbecue. Thread the chicken cubes onto several presoaked wooden skewers, reserving the marinade. Cook the skewers over medium hot coals, turning and brushing frequently with the marinade, for 10 minutes, or until thoroughly cooked. Transfer to a large serving plate and serve immediately.

*these are full of fabulous
mediterranean flavors*

turkey
with cilantro pesto

∙∙∙

serves 4

1 lb/450 g skinless,
  boneless turkey, cut into
  2-inch/5-cm cubes
2 zucchinis, thickly sliced
1 red and 1 yellow bell
  pepper, seeded and cut
  into 2-inch/5-cm squares
8 cherry tomatoes
8 pearl onions, peeled but
  left whole

marinade
6 tbsp olive oil
3 tbsp dry white wine
1 tsp green peppercorns,
  crushed
2 tbsp chopped fresh
  cilantro
salt

cilantro pesto
4 tbsp fresh cilantro leaves
1 tbsp fresh parsley leaves
1 garlic clove
½ cup pine nuts
¼ cup freshly grated
  Parmesan cheese
6 tbsp extra-virgin olive oil
juice of 1 lemon

Place the turkey in a large glass bowl. To make the marinade, mix the olive oil, wine, peppercorns, and cilantro together in a measuring cup and season to taste with salt. Pour the mixture over the turkey and turn until the turkey is thoroughly coated. Cover with plastic wrap and let marinate in the refrigerator for 2 hours.

Preheat the barbecue. To make the pesto, put the cilantro and parsley into a food processor and process until finely chopped. Add the garlic and pine nuts and pulse until chopped. Add the Parmesan cheese, oil, and lemon juice and process briefly to mix. Transfer to a bowl, cover, and let chill in the refrigerator until required.

Drain the turkey, reserving the marinade. Thread the turkey, zucchini slices, bell pepper pieces, cherry tomatoes, and onions alternately onto metal skewers. Cook over medium hot coals, turning and brushing frequently with the marinade, for 10 minutes. Serve immediately with the cilantro pesto.

use any firm white fish for these tasty skewers

caribbean fish
kabobs

∙∙

serves 6

2 lb 4 oz/1 kg swordfish
   steaks
3 tbsp olive oil
3 tbsp lime juice
1 garlic clove, finely
   chopped
1 tsp paprika
salt and pepper
3 onions, cut into wedges
6 tomatoes, cut into
   wedges

Using a sharp knife, cut the fish into 1-inch/2.5-cm cubes and place in a shallow, nonmetallic dish. Place the oil, lime juice, garlic, and paprika in a measuring cup and mix. Season to taste with salt and pepper. Pour the marinade over the fish, turning to coat. Cover with plastic wrap and let marinate in the refrigerator for 1 hour.

Preheat the barbecue. Thread the fish cubes, onion, and tomato wedges alternately onto 6 long, presoaked wooden skewers. Set aside the marinade.

Cook the kabobs over medium hot coals for 8–10 minutes, turning and brushing frequently with the reserved marinade. When they are cooked through, transfer the kabobs to a large serving plate, and serve immediately.

juicy shrimp combined with delicate thai flavors

coconut shrimp

•••

serves 4

6 scallions
1¾ cups coconut milk
finely grated rind and
   juice of 1 lime
4 tbsp chopped fresh
   cilantro, plus extra
   to garnish
2 tbsp corn oil
pepper
1 lb 7 oz/650 g raw jumbo
   shrimp
lemon wedges, to garnish

Finely chop the scallions and place in a large, shallow, nonmetallic dish with the coconut milk, lime rind and juice, cilantro, and oil. Mix well and season to taste with pepper. Add the shrimp, turning to coat. Cover with plastic wrap and let marinate in the refrigerator for 1 hour.

Preheat the barbecue. Drain the shrimp, reserving the marinade. Thread the shrimp onto 8 long metal skewers.

Cook the skewers over medium hot coals, brushing with the reserved marinade and turning frequently, for 8 minutes, or until they have changed color. Serve the shrimp immediately, garnished with the lemon wedges and chopped cilantro.

classic vegetable kabobs with a fruity twist

greek vegetable
kabobs

• •

serves 4

2 onions
8 new potatoes, washed
  but not peeled
salt
1 eggplant, cut into
  8 pieces
8 thick slices cucumber
1 red bell pepper, seeded
  and cut into 8 pieces
1 yellow bell pepper,
  seeded and cut into
  8 pieces
8 oz/225 g provolone
  cheese, cut into 8 cubes
2 nectarines, pitted and
  cut into wedges
8 button mushrooms
2 tbsp olive oil
2 tsp chopped fresh thyme
2 tsp chopped fresh
  rosemary
1 quantity cucumber
  and yogurt dip
  (see page 180), to serve

Preheat the barbecue. Cut the onions into wedges, then place the onions and potatoes in a pan of lightly salted boiling water and cook for 20 minutes, or until just tender. Drain and let cool. Meanwhile, blanch the eggplant in boiling water for 2 minutes, then add the cucumber and let simmer for 1 minute. Add the bell peppers and let simmer for 2 minutes, then drain and let the vegetables cool.

Place the cooled vegetables, cheese, nectarines, and mushrooms in a bowl. Add the olive oil and herbs and toss to coat. Thread the vegetables, cheese, nectarines, and mushrooms onto several metal skewers.

Cook the kabobs over hot coals, turning frequently, for 15 minutes. Transfer to a large serving plate and serve immediately with the cucumber and yogurt dip.

these kabobs are perfect for any vegetarian guests

marinated tofu
skewers

••

serves 4

12 oz/350 g firm tofu
1 red bell pepper
1 yellow bell pepper
2 zucchini
8 button mushrooms

marinade
grated rind and
  juice of ½ lemon
1 garlic clove, crushed
½ tsp chopped fresh
  rosemary
½ tsp chopped fresh
  thyme
1 tbsp walnut oil

to garnish
shredded carrot
lemon wedges

To make the marinade, mix the lemon rind and juice, garlic, rosemary, thyme, and walnut oil together in a shallow dish. Drain the tofu, pat it dry on paper towels, and cut it into squares. Add to the marinade and toss to coat. Let marinate for 20–30 minutes.

Preheat the barbecue. Seed the bell peppers and cut into 1-inch/2.5-cm pieces. Blanch in boiling water for 4 minutes, refresh in cold water, and drain. Using a channel knife or potato peeler, remove strips of peel from the zucchini. Cut the zucchini into 1-inch/2.5-cm chunks.

Remove the tofu from the marinade, reserving the liquid for basting. Thread the tofu onto 8 presoaked wooden skewers, alternating with the bell peppers, zucchini, and mushrooms.

Cook the skewers over medium hot coals for 6 minutes, turning and basting with the marinade. Transfer the skewers to warmed serving plates, garnish with shredded carrot and lemon wedges, and serve.

Sides
& Sauces

a deliciously irresistible side dish

crispy potato skins

serves 4–6

8 small baking potatoes,
   scrubbed
1¾ oz/50 g butter, melted
salt and pepper

optional topping
6 scallions, sliced
½ cup grated Gruyère
   cheese
1¾ oz/50 g salami,
   cut into thin strips

Preheat the oven to 400°F/200°C. Prick the potatoes with a fork and bake in the oven for 1 hour, or until tender. Alternatively, cook in a microwave on High for 12–15 minutes. Cut the potatoes in half and scoop out the flesh, leaving about ¼ inch/5 mm potato flesh lining the skin.

Preheat the barbecue. Brush the insides of the potatoes with melted butter.

Place the skins, cut-side down, over medium hot coals and cook for 10–15 minutes. Turn the potato skins over and cook for an additional 5 minutes, or until they are crispy. Take care that they do not burn. Season the potato skins with salt and pepper to taste and serve while they are still warm.

If desired, the skins can be filled with a variety of toppings. Grill the potato skins as above for 10 minutes, then turn cut-side up and sprinkle with slices of scallion, grated cheese, and chopped salami. Cook for an additional 5 minutes, or until the cheese begins to melt. Serve hot.

barbecuing transforms potatoes into tempting treats

potato fans

serves 6

6 large potatoes, scrubbed
  but not peeled
1 garlic clove, finely
  chopped
2 tbsp olive oil
salt and pepper

Preheat the barbecue. Using a sharp knife, make a series of cuts across the potatoes almost all the way through. Cut out 6 squares of foil, each large enough to enclose a potato, and place a potato on top of each one.

Mix together the garlic and olive oil and brush generously over the potatoes. Season with salt and pepper to taste. Fold up the sides of the foil to enclose the potatoes completely.

Cook over hot coals, turning occasionally, for 1 hour. To serve, open the foil packages and gently pinch the potatoes to open up the fans.

pumpkin packages
with chile & lime

serves 4

1 lb 9 oz/700 g pumpkin
   or squash
2 tbsp corn oil
1 oz/25 g butter
½ tsp chili sauce
grated rind of 1 lime
2 tsp lime juice

Preheat the barbecue. Halve the pumpkin or squash and scoop out the seeds. Rinse the seeds and reserve. Cut the pumpkin into thin wedges and peel.

Heat the corn oil and butter together in a large pan, stirring, until melted. Stir in the chili sauce, lime rind, and juice. Add the pumpkin and seeds to the pan and toss to coat on all sides in the flavored butter.

Divide the mixture among 4 double-thickness sheets of aluminum foil. Fold over the foil to enclose the pumpkin mixture completely.

Cook the foil packages over hot coals for 15–25 minutes, or until the pumpkin is tender. Transfer the packages to warmed serving plates. To serve, open the packages at the table.

a classic accompaniment, barbecue-style

garlic bread

serves 6

5½ oz/150 g butter, softened
3 garlic cloves, crushed
2 tbsp chopped fresh parsley
pepper
1 large or 2 small loaves of French bread

Mix together the butter, garlic, and parsley in a bowl until well combined. Season with pepper to taste and mix well.

Cut a few lengthwise slits in the French bread. Spread the flavored butter inside the slits and place the bread on a large sheet of thick aluminum foil.

Preheat the barbecue. Wrap the bread well in the foil and cook over hot coals for 10–15 minutes, until the butter melts and the bread is piping hot.

Serve as an accompaniment to a wide range of dishes.

juicy corn cobs with a delicious herb butter

corn on the cob

serves 4

4 corn cobs, with husks
3½ oz/100 g butter
1 tbsp chopped fresh
   parsley
1 tsp chopped fresh chives
1 tsp chopped fresh thyme
grated rind of 1 lemon
salt and pepper

Preheat the barbecue. To prepare the corn cobs, peel back the husks and remove the silk. Fold the husks back around the kernels and secure them in place with string if necessary.

Blanch the corn cobs in a large pan of boiling water for 5 minutes. Remove with a slotted spoon and drain thoroughly. Cook the corn cobs over medium hot coals for 20–30 minutes, turning frequently.

Meanwhile, soften the butter and beat in the parsley, chives, thyme, lemon rind, and salt and pepper to taste. Transfer the corn cobs to serving plates, remove the string, and pull back the husks. Serve each with a generous portion of herb butter.

charbroiled vegetables with creamy pesto

serves 4

1 red onion
1 fennel bulb
4 baby eggplants
4 baby zucchini
1 orange bell pepper
1 red bell pepper
2 beefsteak tomatoes
2 tbsp olive oil
salt and pepper
1 fresh basil sprig,
   to garnish

creamy pesto
4 tbsp fresh basil leaves
1 tbsp pine nuts
1 garlic clove
pinch of coarse sea salt
¼ cup freshly grated
   Parmesan cheese
¼ cup extra-virgin
   olive oil
⅔ cup strained plain
   yogurt

Preheat the barbecue. To make the creamy pesto, place the basil, pine nuts, garlic, and sea salt in a mortar and pound to a paste with a pestle. Gradually work in the Parmesan cheese, then gradually stir in the oil.

Place the yogurt in a small serving bowl and stir in 3–4 tablespoons of the pesto mixture. Cover with plastic wrap and let chill in the refrigerator until required. Store any leftover pesto mixture in a screw-top jar in the refrigerator.

Prepare the vegetables. Cut the onion and fennel bulb into wedges, trim and slice the eggplants and zucchini, seed and thickly slice the bell peppers, and cut the tomatoes in half. Brush the vegetables with oil and season to taste with salt and pepper.

Cook the eggplants and bell peppers over hot coals for 3 minutes, then add the zucchini, onion, fennel, and tomatoes and cook, turning occasionally and brushing with more oil if necessary, for an additional 5 minutes. Transfer to a large serving plate and serve with the pesto, garnished with a basil sprig.

use your favorite baby vegetables in these packages

summer vegetable
packages

· ·

serves 4

2 lb 4 oz/1 kg mixed baby
   vegetables, such as
   carrots, asparagus, baby
   corn, cherry tomatoes,
   leeks, zucchini, chiles,
   and onions
1 lemon
4 oz/115 g unsalted butter
3 tbsp chopped mixed
   fresh herbs, such as
   parsley, thyme, chives,
   and chervil
2 garlic cloves
salt and pepper

Preheat the barbecue. Cut out 4 x 12-inch/30-cm squares of foil and divide the vegetables equally among them.

Using a grater, finely grate the lemon rind, then squeeze the juice from the lemon and set aside until required. Put the lemon rind, butter, herbs, and garlic into a food processor and process until blended, then season to taste with salt and pepper. Alternatively, beat together in a bowl until blended.

Divide the butter equally among the vegetables, dotting it on top. Fold up the sides of the foil to enclose the vegetables, sealing securely. Cook over medium hot coals, turning occasionally, for 25–30 minutes. Open the packages, sprinkle with the reserved lemon juice, and serve immediately.

tropical rice salad

serves 4

½ cup long-grain rice
salt and pepper
4 scallions
8 oz/225 g canned
  pineapple chunks in
  natural juice
7 oz/200 g canned corn,
  drained
2 red bell peppers, seeded
  and diced
3 tbsp golden raisins

dressing
1 tbsp peanut oil
1 tbsp hazelnut oil
1 tbsp light soy sauce
1 garlic clove, finely
  chopped
1 tsp chopped fresh
  gingerroot

Cook the rice in a large pan of lightly salted boiling water for 15 minutes, or until tender. Drain thoroughly and rinse under cold running water. Place the rice in a large serving bowl.

Using a sharp knife, finely chop the scallions. Drain the pineapple chunks, reserving the juice in a measuring cup. Add the pineapple chunks, corn, red bell peppers, chopped scallions, and golden raisins to the rice and mix lightly.

Add all the dressing ingredients to the reserved pineapple juice, whisking well, and season to taste with salt and pepper. Pour the dressing over the salad and toss until the salad is thoroughly coated. Serve immediately.

make this salad a day ahead and leave to infuse

tabbouleh

serves 4

1 cup bulgur wheat
3 tbsp extra-virgin olive oil
4 tbsp lemon juice
salt and pepper
4 scallions
1 green bell pepper, seeded
  and sliced
4 tomatoes, chopped
2 tbsp chopped fresh
  parsley
2 tbsp chopped fresh mint
8 black olives, pitted
fresh mint sprigs,
  to garnish

Place the bulgur wheat in a large bowl and add enough cold water to cover. Let stand for 30 minutes, or until the wheat has doubled in size. Drain well and press out as much liquid as possible. Spread out the wheat on paper towels to dry.

Place the wheat in a serving bowl. Mix the olive oil and lemon juice together in a measuring cup and season to taste with salt and pepper. Pour the lemon mixture over the wheat and let marinate for 1 hour.

Using a sharp knife, finely chop the scallions, then add to the salad with the green bell pepper, tomatoes, parsley, and mint, and toss lightly to mix. Top the salad with the olives and garnish with fresh mint sprigs, then serve.

pasta salad
with basil vinaigrette

serves 4

8 oz/225 g dried fusilli
salt and pepper
4 tomatoes
scant ⅓ cup black olives
1 oz/25 g sun-dried
   tomatoes in oil
2 tbsp pine nuts
2 tbsp freshly grated
   Parmesan cheese
fresh basil leaves,
   to garnish

vinaigrette
½ oz/15 g basil leaves
1 garlic clove, crushed
2 tbsp freshly grated
   Parmesan cheese
4 tbsp extra-virgin olive oil
2 tbsp lemon juice

Cook the pasta in a large pan of lightly salted boiling water for 10–12 minutes, or until just tender but still firm to the bite. Drain the pasta, rinse under cold running water, then drain again thoroughly. Place the pasta in a large bowl.

Preheat the broiler to medium. To make the vinaigrette, place the basil leaves, garlic, cheese, olive oil, and lemon juice in a food processor. Season to taste with salt and pepper and process until the leaves are well chopped and the ingredients are combined. Alternatively, finely chop the basil leaves by hand and combine with the other vinaigrette ingredients. Pour the vinaigrette over the pasta and toss to coat.

Cut the tomatoes into wedges. Pit and halve the olives. Slice the sun-dried tomatoes. Toast the pine nuts on a cookie sheet under the hot broiler until golden.

Add the tomatoes (fresh and sun-dried) and the olives to the pasta and mix until combined.

Transfer the pasta to a serving dish, sprinkle over the Parmesan and toasted pine nuts and serve garnished with a few basil leaves.

a classic, flavorful Italian bread salad

panzanella

· ·

serves 4–6

9 oz/250 g stale focaccia,
   ciabatta, or French bread
4 large, vine-ripened
   tomatoes
about 6 tbsp extra-virgin
   olive oil
4 red, yellow, and/or
   orange bell peppers
3½ oz/100 g cucumber
1 large red onion, finely
   chopped
8 canned anchovy fillets,
   drained and chopped
2 tbsp capers in brine,
   rinsed and patted dry
about 4 tbsp red wine
   vinegar
about 2 tbsp best-quality
   balsamic vinegar
salt and pepper
fresh basil leaves,
   to garnish

Cut the bread into 1-inch/2.5-cm cubes and place in a large bowl. Working over a plate to catch any juices, quarter the tomatoes; reserve the juices. Using a teaspoon, scoop out the cores and seeds and discard, then finely chop the flesh. Add to the bread cubes.

Drizzle 5 tablespoons of the olive oil over the mixture and toss with your hands until well coated. Pour in the reserved tomato juice and toss again. Set aside for about 30 minutes.

Meanwhile, cut the bell peppers in half and remove the cores and seeds. Place on a metal rack under a preheated hot broiler and broil for 10 minutes, or until the skins are charred and the flesh softened. Place in a plastic bag, seal, and set aside for 20 minutes to allow the steam to loosen the skins. Remove the skins, then finely chop.

Cut the cucumber in half lengthwise, then cut each half into 3 strips lengthwise. Using a teaspoon, scoop out and discard the seeds. Dice the cucumber.

Add the onion, peppers, cucumber, anchovy fillets, and capers to the bread and toss together. Sprinkle with the red wine and balsamic vinegars and season to taste with salt and pepper. Drizzle with extra olive oil or vinegar if necessary, but be cautious that it does not become too greasy or soggy. Sprinkle the fresh basil leaves over the salad and serve at once.

spinach & orange
salad

serves 4–6

8 oz/225 g baby spinach
  leaves
2 large oranges
½ red onion

dressing
3 tbsp extra-virgin olive oil
2 tbsp freshly squeezed
  orange juice
2 tsp lemon juice
1 tsp clear honey
½ tsp whole-grain
  mustard
salt and pepper

Wash the spinach leaves under cold running water and dry them thoroughly on paper towels. Remove and discard any tough stems and tear the larger leaves into smaller pieces.

Slice the top and bottom off each orange with a sharp knife, then remove the peel. Carefully slice between the membranes of the orange to remove the segments.

Using a sharp knife, finely chop the onion. Mix the salad greens and orange segments together and arrange in a serving dish. Scatter the chopped onion over the salad.

To make the dressing, whisk the olive oil, orange juice, lemon juice, honey, mustard, and salt and pepper to taste together in a small bowl. Pour the dressing over the salad just before serving. Toss the salad well to coat the greens with the dressing.

tangy feta cheese and green beans are a great mix

green bean & feta
salad

. . . .

serves 4

12 oz/350 g green beans, trimmed
1 red onion, chopped
3–4 tbsp chopped fresh cilantro
2 radishes, thinly sliced
¾ cup crumbled feta cheese
1 tsp chopped fresh oregano or ½ tsp dried oregano
pepper
2 tbsp red wine or fruit vinegar
5 tbsp extra-virgin olive oil
6 ripe cherry or small tomatoes, quartered

Bring about 2 inches/5 cm of water to a boil in the base of a steamer or in a medium saucepan. Add the green beans to the top of the steamer or place them in a metal colander set over the pan of water. Cover and steam for about 5 minutes until just tender.

Transfer the beans to a bowl and add the onion, cilantro, radishes, and crumbled feta cheese.

Sprinkle the oregano over the salad, then grind pepper over to taste. Whisk the vinegar and olive oil together and then pour over the salad. Toss gently to mix well.

Transfer to a serving platter, surround with the tomato quarters, and serve at once or chill until ready to serve.

the perfect addition to any barbecue menu

potato salad

· ·

serves 4

1 lb 9 oz/700 g tiny new
  potatoes
8 scallions
1 hard-cooked egg
  (optional)
1 cup mayonnaise
1 tsp paprika
salt and pepper

to garnish
2 tbsp snipped fresh
  chives
pinch of paprika

Bring a large pan of lightly salted water to a boil. Add the potatoes and cook for 10–15 minutes, or until just tender.

Drain the potatoes and rinse them under cold running water until completely cold. Drain again. Transfer the potatoes to a bowl and reserve until required. Using a sharp knife, slice the scallions thinly on the diagonal. Chop the hard-cooked egg, if using.

Mix the mayonnaise, paprika, and salt and pepper to taste together in a bowl. Pour the mixture over the potatoes. Add the scallions and egg, if using, to the potatoes and toss together.

Transfer the potato salad to a serving bowl and sprinkle with snipped chives and a pinch of paprika. Cover and let chill in the refrigerator until required.

coleslaw

serves 10–12

⅔ cup mayonnaise
⅔ cup lowfat plain yogurt
dash of Tabasco sauce
salt and pepper
1 medium head of white
    cabbage
4 carrots
1 green bell pepper

To make the dressing, mix the mayonnaise, yogurt, Tabasco sauce, and salt and pepper to taste together in a small bowl. Chill in the refrigerator until required.

Cut the cabbage in half and then into quarters. Remove and discard the tough center stem. Shred the cabbage leaves finely. Wash the leaves under cold running water and dry thoroughly on paper towels. Peel the carrots and shred in a food processor or on a mandoline. Alternatively, roughly grate the carrot. Cut the bell pepper into quarters, then seed it and cut the flesh into thin strips.

Mix the vegetables together in a large serving bowl and toss to mix. Pour over the dressing and toss until the vegetables are well coated. Let the vegetable mixture chill until required.

homemade mayonnaise is far superior to store-bought

mayonnaise

makes about 1¼ cups

2 large egg yolks
2 tsp Dijon mustard
¾ tsp salt, or to taste
white pepper
2 tbsp lemon juice or white
    wine vinegar
about 1¼ cups
    sunflower oil

Blend the egg yolks with the Dijon mustard, salt, and white pepper to taste in a food processor or blender or by hand. Add the lemon juice and blend again.

With the motor still running or still beating, add the oil, drop by drop at first. When the sauce begins to thicken, add the oil in a slow, steady stream. Taste and adjust the seasoning with extra salt, pepper, and lemon juice, if necessary. If the sauce seems too thick, slowly add 1 tablespoon hot water, light cream, or lemon juice.

Use at once or store in an airtight container in the refrigerator for up to 1 week.

a garlic-infused variation on classic mayonnaise

aïoli

makes about 1 cup

3 large garlic cloves,
   finely chopped
2 egg yolks
1 cup extra-virgin olive oil
1 tbsp lemon juice
1 tbsp lime juice
1 tbsp Dijon mustard
1 tbsp chopped fresh
   tarragon
salt and pepper
1 fresh tarragon sprig,
   to garnish

Make sure all the ingredients are at room temperature. Place the garlic and egg yolks in a food processor and process until well blended. With the motor running, pour in the oil, teaspoon by teaspoon, through the feeder tube until the mixture starts to thicken, then pour in the remaining oil in a thin stream until a thick mayonnaise forms.

Add the lemon and lime juices, mustard, and tarragon and season to taste with salt and pepper. Blend until smooth, then transfer to a nonmetallic bowl. Garnish with a tarragon sprig. Cover with plastic wrap and let chill until required.

this is a cool and fresh-tasting dip

cucumber &
yogurt dip

serves 4

1 small cucumber
1¼ cups strained plain
  yogurt
1 large garlic clove,
  crushed
1 tbsp chopped fresh mint
  or dill
salt and pepper
warm pita bread, to serve

Peel then coarsely grate the cucumber. Put in a strainer and squeeze out as much of the water as possible. Put the cucumber into a bowl.

Add the yogurt, garlic, and chopped mint (reserve a little as a garnish, if desired) to the cucumber and season with pepper. Mix well together and chill in the refrigerator for about 2 hours before serving.

To serve, stir the cucumber and yogurt dip and transfer to a serving bowl. Sprinkle with salt and accompany with warmed pita bread.

a well-loved, healthy, and delicious dip

chickpea &
sesame dip

serves 8

8 oz/225 g dried
  chickpeas, covered
  with water and soaked
  overnight
juice of 2 large lemons
⅔ cup tahini paste
2 garlic cloves, crushed
4 tbsp extra-virgin olive oil
small pinch of ground
  cumin
salt and pepper
warm pita bread, to serve

to garnish
1 tsp paprika
chopped flat-leaf parsley

Drain the chickpeas, put in a saucepan, and cover with cold water. Bring to a boil, then simmer for about 2 hours, until very tender.

Drain the chickpeas, reserving a little of the liquid, and put in a food processor, reserving a few to garnish. Blend the chickpeas until smooth, gradually adding the lemon juice and enough reserved liquid to form a smooth, thick purée. Add the tahini paste, garlic, 3 tablespoons of the olive oil, and the cumin and blend until smooth. Season with salt and pepper.

Turn the mixture into a shallow serving dish and chill in the refrigerator for 2–3 hours before serving. To serve, mix the reserved olive oil with the paprika and drizzle over the top of the dish. Sprinkle with the parsley and the reserved chickpeas. Accompany with warm pita bread.

a tangy dip full of vibrant summer flavors

guacamole

serves 4

2 large, ripe avocados
juice of 1 lime, or to taste
2 tsp olive oil
½ onion, finely chopped
1 fresh green chile, such
  as poblano, seeded and
  finely chopped
1 garlic clove, crushed
¼ tsp ground cumin
1 tbsp chopped fresh
  cilantro
salt and pepper
tortilla chips, to serve
fresh dill or cilantro
  sprigs, to garnish

Cut the avocados in half lengthwise and twist the 2 halves in opposite directions to separate. Stab the pit with the point of a sharp knife and lift out.

Peel, then coarsely chop the avocado halves and place in a non-metallic bowl. Squeeze over the lime juice and add the oil. Mash the avocados with a fork until the desired consistency is achieved—either chunky or smooth. Blend in the onion, chile, garlic, cumin, and chopped cilantro, then season to taste with salt and pepper.

Transfer to a serving dish and serve at once, to avoid discoloration, with tortilla chips and garnished with fresh dill sprigs.

tomato salsa

serves 6

1 lb/450 g firm,
  ripe tomatoes
1 fresh jalapeño or other
  small hot chile
2 tsp extra-virgin olive oil
1 garlic clove, crushed
grated rind and juice
  of 1 lime
pinch of sugar
4 tbsp chopped cilantro
salt
cilantro sprigs, to garnish

Using a sharp knife, finely dice the tomatoes and put into a bowl with the seeds. Halve the chile, remove and discard the seeds, and very finely dice the flesh. Add to the tomatoes.

Add all the remaining ingredients to the tomatoes, season to taste with salt, and mix well together.

Turn the mixture into a small, nonmetallic serving bowl, cover, and leave at room temperature for 30 minutes to let the flavors combine. If not being served right away, the salsa can be stored in the refrigerator for up to 2–3 days, but it is best if allowed to return to room temperature for 1 hour before being served. Serve garnished with cilantro sprigs.

a popular accompaniment to burgers and meats

roasted
bell pepper relish

serves 6–8

1 each of yellow, red, and
  green bell peppers
1 tbsp extra-virgin olive oil
½ tsp brown sugar
1 tsp balsamic vinegar
¼ tsp salt
¼ tsp paprika

Preheat the broiler to medium. Put the bell peppers onto a broiler rack and cook, turning frequently, for 15 minutes, or until the skins are charred all over.

Transfer the bell peppers to a bowl, then immediately cover with a clean, damp dish towel and leave for at least 2 hours, or overnight, until cold.

When the bell peppers are cold, hold them over a clean bowl to collect the juices and peel off the skin. Remove and discard the stem, core, and seeds and finely dice the flesh.

Add the diced bell peppers to the juices in the bowl, then add the oil, sugar, vinegar, salt, and paprika. Stir together until well mixed, and serve, or store in an airtight container in the refrigerator for up to 4–5 days.

homemade
tomato sauce

. . . .

makes about 2 cups

1 tbsp butter
2 tbsp olive oil
1 onion, chopped
1 garlic clove, finely
   chopped
14 oz/400 g canned
   tomatoes or 1 lb/450 g
   fresh tomatoes, peeled
1 tbsp tomato paste
generous ½ cup red wine
⅔ cup vegetable stock
½ tsp sugar
1 bay leaf
salt and pepper

Melt the butter with the oil in a large pan over medium heat, add the onion and garlic, and cook, stirring frequently, for 5 minutes, or until the onion has softened and is beginning to brown.

Add all the remaining ingredients to the pan and season to taste with salt and pepper. Bring to a boil, then reduce the heat to low and let simmer, uncovered and stirring occasionally, for 30 minutes, or until the tomato sauce has thickened.

Remove and discard the bay leaf, pour the sauce into a food processor or blender, and process until smooth. Alternatively, using the back of a wooden spoon, push the sauce through a nylon strainer into a bowl.

If serving at once, reheat the sauce gently in a pan. Alternatively, store and reheat before serving.

no barbecue meal would be complete without it

spicy bbq sauce

serves 4

2 tbsp corn oil
1 large onion, chopped
2 garlic cloves, chopped
1 cup canned chopped
  tomatoes
1 tbsp Worcestershire
  sauce
2 tbsp fruity brown sauce
2 tbsp brown sugar
4 tbsp white wine vinegar
½ tsp mild chili powder
¼ tsp dry mustard
dash of Tabasco sauce
salt and pepper
cooked sausages or
  burgers in bread rolls,
  to serve

To make the sauce, heat the oil in a small pan and cook the onion and garlic for 4–5 minutes, or until softened and just beginning to brown.

Add the tomatoes, Worcestershire sauce, brown sauce, sugar, vinegar, chili powder, dry mustard, and Tabasco sauce to the pan. Add salt and pepper to taste, and bring to a boil.

Reduce the heat and simmer gently for 10–15 minutes, or until the sauce begins to thicken slightly. Stir occasionally so that the sauce does not burn and stick to the bottom of the pan. Set aside and keep warm until required. Serve with sausages or burgers.

Desserts & Drinks

toffee fruit kabobs

serves 4

2 apples, cored and cut
   into wedges
2 firm pears, cored and
   cut into wedges
juice of ½ lemon
2 tbsp brown sugar
¼ tsp ground allspice
1 oz/25 g unsalted butter,
   melted

sauce
4½ oz/125 g butter
½ cup brown sugar
6 tbsp heavy cream

Preheat the barbecue. Toss the apples and pears in the lemon juice to prevent any discoloration.

Mix the sugar and allspice together and sprinkle over the fruit. Thread the fruit pieces onto skewers.

To make the toffee sauce, place the butter and sugar in a pan and heat, stirring gently, until the butter has melted and the sugar has dissolved.

Add the cream to the pan and bring to a boil. Boil for 1–2 minutes, then let cool slightly.

Meanwhile, place the fruit kabobs over hot coals and cook for 5 minutes, turning and basting frequently with the melted butter, until the fruit is just tender. Transfer the fruit kabobs to warmed serving plates and serve with the cooled toffee sauce.

bananas lend themselves perfectly to barbecuing

chocolate rum bananas

∙∙

serves 4

1 tbsp butter
8 oz/225 g semisweet or
  milk chocolate
4 large bananas
2 tbsp rum
sour cream, mascarpone
  cheese, or ice cream,
  to serve
grated nutmeg,
  to decorate

Take four 10-inch/25-cm squares of aluminum foil and brush them with butter.

Grate the chocolate. Make a careful slit lengthwise in the peel of each banana, and open just wide enough to insert the chocolate. Place the grated chocolate inside the bananas, along their lengths, then close them up.

Wrap each stuffed banana in a square of foil, then barbecue them over hot coals for about 5–10 minutes, or until the chocolate has melted inside the bananas. Remove from the barbecue, place the bananas on individual serving plates, and pour some rum into each banana.

Serve at once with sour cream, mascarpone cheese, or ice cream, topped with nutmeg.

mascarpone
peaches

. . . .

serves 4

4 peaches
6 oz/175 g mascarpone
   cheese
1½ oz/40 g pecans or
   walnuts, chopped
1 tsp corn oil
4 tbsp maple syrup

Cut the peaches in half and remove the pits. If you are preparing this recipe in advance, press the peach halves together and wrap in plastic wrap until required.

Mix the mascarpone cheese and pecans together in a bowl until well combined. Leave to chill in the refrigerator until required. Preheat the barbecue. Brush the peach halves with a little corn oil and place on a rack set over medium hot coals. Cook the peach halves for 5–10 minutes, turning once, until hot.

Transfer the peach halves to a serving dish and top with the mascarpone and nut mixture. Drizzle the maple syrup over the peaches and mascarpone filling and serve immediately.

fresh pineapple and rum are a magical combination

totally tropical

pineapple

∙∙∙

serves 4

1 pineapple
3 tbsp dark rum
2 tbsp brown sugar
1 tsp ground ginger
2 oz/55 g unsalted butter,
  melted

Preheat the barbecue. Using a sharp knife, cut off the crown of the pineapple, then cut the fruit into ¾-inch/2-cm thick slices. Cut away the peel from each slice and flick out the "eyes" with the tip of the knife. Stamp out the cores with an apple corer or small cookie cutter.

Mix the rum, sugar, ginger, and butter together in a measuring cup, stirring constantly, until the sugar has dissolved. Brush the pineapple rings with the rum mixture.

Cook the pineapple rings over hot coals for 3–4 minutes on each side. Transfer to serving plates and serve immediately with the remaining rum mixture poured over them.

succulent figs with melting cheese and cinnamon

stuffed figs

serves 4

8 fresh figs
scant ½ cup cream cheese
1 tsp ground cinnamon
3 tbsp brown sugar
plain yogurt, sour cream,
    mascarpone cheese, or
    ice cream, to serve

Cut out eight 7-inch/18-cm squares of aluminum foil. Make a small slit in each fig, then place each fig on a square of foil.

Put the cream cheese in a bowl. Add the cinnamon and stir until well combined. Stuff the inside of each fig with the cinnamon cream cheese, then sprinkle a teaspoon of sugar over each one. Close the foil round each fig to make a package.

Place the packages on the barbecue and cook over hot coals, turning them frequently, for about 10 minutes, or until the figs are cooked to your taste.

Transfer the figs to serving plates and serve at once with plain yogurt, sour cream, mascarpone cheese, or ice cream.

a delicious treat to end any barbecued meal

panettone with mascarpone & strawberries

··

serves 4

8 oz/225 g strawberries
2 tbsp superfine sugar
6 tbsp Marsala wine
½ tsp ground cinnamon
4 slices panettone
4 tbsp mascarpone cheese

Hull and slice the strawberries and place them in a bowl. Add the sugar, Marsala, and cinnamon to the strawberries.

Toss the strawberries in the sugar and cinnamon mixture until they are well coated. Let chill in the refrigerator for at least 30 minutes. Preheat the barbecue. When ready to serve, transfer the slices of panettone to a rack set over medium hot coals. Cook the panettone for 1 minute on each side, or until golden brown.

Remove the panettone from the barbecue and transfer to serving plates. Top the panettone with the mascarpone cheese and the marinated strawberries. Serve immediately.

tasty fruit chunks in a honey-liqueur sauce

mixed fruit kabobs

· ·

serves 4

2 nectarines, halved and
   pitted
2 kiwis
4 red plums
1 mango, peeled, halved,
   and pitted
2 bananas, peeled and
   thickly sliced
8 strawberries, hulled
1 tbsp honey
3 tbsp Cointreau

Cut the nectarine halves into wedges and place in a large, shallow dish. Peel and quarter the kiwis. Cut the plums in half and remove the pits. Cut the mango flesh into chunks and add to the dish with the kiwis, plums, bananas, and strawberries.

Mix the honey and Cointreau together in a measuring cup until blended. Pour the mixture over the fruit and toss to coat. Cover with plastic wrap and let marinate in the refrigerator for 1 hour.

Preheat the barbecue. Drain the fruit, reserving the marinade. Thread the fruit onto several presoaked wooden skewers and cook over medium hot coals, turning and brushing frequently with the reserved marinade, for 5–7 minutes, then serve.

this well-loved cooler is a traditional favorite

fresh lemonade

• •

serves 4

4 large lemons, preferably
    unwaxed or organic
scant 1 cup superfine
    sugar
3½ cups boiling water
ice cubes, to serve

Scrub the lemons well and dry. Using a vegetable peeler, peel 3 of the lemons very thinly. Place the peel in a large pitcher or bowl, add the sugar and boiling water, and stir well until the sugar has dissolved. Cover the pitcher and let stand for at least 3 hours, stirring occasionally. Meanwhile, squeeze the juice from the 3 lemons and set aside.

Strain the lemon peel and stir in the reserved lemon juice. Thinly slice the remaining lemon and cut the slices in half. Add to the lemonade together with the ice cubes. Stir and serve.

a nonalcoholic version of the classic
Spanish drink

soft sangria

∙ ∙

serves 8

6 cups red grape juice
1¼ cups orange juice
3 measures cranberry juice
2 measures lemon juice
2 measures lime juice
4 measures sugar syrup
ice cubes

to decorate
slices of lemon
slices of orange
slices of lime

Put the grape juice, orange juice, cranberry juice, lemon juice, lime juice, and sugar syrup into a chilled punch bowl and stir well.

Add the ice and decorate with the slices of lemon, orange, and lime.

orange & lime
iced tea

· ·

serves 2

1 ¼ cups water
2 tea bags
scant ½ cup orange juice
4 tbsp lime juice
1–2 tbsp brown sugar
8 ice cubes

to decorate
wedge of lime
granulated sugar
slices of fresh orange,
   lemon, or lime

Pour the water into a pan and bring to a boil. Remove from the heat, add the tea bags, and let stand for 5 minutes to infuse. Remove the tea bags and let the tea cool to room temperature (about 30 minutes). Transfer to a pitcher, cover with plastic wrap, and chill in the refrigerator for at least 45 minutes.

When the tea has chilled, pour in the orange juice and lime juice. Add sugar to taste.

Take two glasses and rub the rims with a wedge of lime, then dip them in granulated sugar to frost. Put the ice cubes into the glasses and pour over the tea. Decorate with slices of fresh orange, lemon, or lime and serve.

an irresistibly attractive adult-only cocktail

singapore sling

· ·

serves 1

10–12 cracked ice cubes
2 measures gin
1 measure cherry brandy
1 measure lemon juice
1 tsp grenadine
soda water, to top off

to decorate
lime peel
cocktail cherries

Put 4–6 cracked ice cubes into a cocktail shaker. Pour the gin, cherry brandy, lemon juice, and grenadine over the ice. Shake vigorously until a frost forms.

Half fill a chilled highball glass with cracked ice cubes and strain the cocktail over them. Top off with soda water and then decorate with a twist of lime peel and cocktail cherries.

a classic combination of tequila, triple sec, and lime

margarita

· ·

serves 1

lime wedge
coarse salt
4–6 cracked ice cubes
3 measures white tequila
1 measure triple sec
2 measures lime juice
slice of lime, to decorate

Rub the rim of a chilled cocktail glass with the lime wedge and then dip in a saucer of coarse salt to frost.

Put the cracked ice cubes into a cocktail shaker. Pour the tequila, triple sec, and lime juice over the ice. Shake vigorously until a frost forms.

Strain into the prepared glass and decorate with the lime slice.

a cooling and refreshing drink with
a kick

club mojito

• •

serves 1

1 tsp simple syrup
a few fresh mint leaves
juice of ½ lime
ice cubes
2 measures Jamaican rum
soda water, to top off

Put the syrup, mint leaves, and lime juice in a highball glass and crush or break apart the mint leaves.

Add ice and rum, then top off with soda water to taste.

index

succulent

tempting

blazing

grilled

scorching

flavors